W9-BIP-994

ISLAM: THE ALTERNATIVE

Third Printing
1419 AH / 1999 AC

Murad Hofmann

Islam: The Alternative

(second enlarged edition)

Translated from German by
Dr. Christiane Banerji and
Murad Hofmann

Foreword by
Annemarie Schimmel

amana publications
Beltsville, Maryland

© 1992 by Murad Hofmann
First published in Germany by Eugen Diederlichs Verlag
First English edition © 1993 Garnet Publishing Ltd, UK
This North American edition is published by (amana publications)
by arrangement with Garnet Publishing Ltd.

Second enlarged edition
amana publications
10710 Tucker Street
Beltsville, Maryland 20705-2223 USA
Tel: (301)595-5777   Fax: (301)595-5888
E-mail: igamana@erols.com Website: www.amana-publications.com

Library of Congress Cataloging-in-Publication Data

Hofmann, Murad Wilfried. (1931 AC/1349 AH) –
    [Islam als Alternative.   English]
    Islam : the alternative 2nd Enlarged Edition / Murad Hofmann.
    Translated from German by Dr. Christiane Banerji and Murad Hofmann
        p. 192   cm. 23
    Originally published: Reading : Garnet, 1993.
    Includes bibliographical references (p. 161–172) and index.

    ISBN 0-915957-66-3

    1. Islam—Apologetic works.

BP170.H6413   1997
297.2'9—dc21   97–18601
                                                                   CIP

Printed in the United States of America by International Graphics
10710 Tucker Street, Beltsville, Maryland 20705-2223-USA
Tel: (301) 595-5999 Fax: (301) 595-5888
Email: igfx@aol.com

CONTENTS

PREFACE TO THE SECOND EDITION

In 1991, while I was in the lush Moroccan oasis of Taroudant, just south of the High Atlas mountains, the idea suddenly struck me that Francis Fukuyama's notion of the imminent 'end of history'[1] was crying out for a strong reply—historically sound, scientifically honest, problem-conscious, and free from apologetics—a reply pointing out that there is an alternative to cultural monotony: Islam—not only as a viable option, but as the only alternative to an Occident that is increasingly troubled by social and ideological crises. Two months later, this book was ready.

The idea that, following the collapse of communism, the world was to become one-dimensional impressed me as misguided triumphalism, as a misjudgment typical of what 'Third World' people denounce as cultural imperialism: the eager expectation that sooner or later—rather sooner than later—the 'project of modernity' (profanely known as the 'American Way of Life') was to become the obligatory model for all other societies around the globe—as if there was no alternative left. Not much later, Samuel Huntington enlarged on this naive idea by implying more concretely that the Muslim world was bound to disappear or to become fully marginalized[2] —a prejudice traceable back to European thinking of the Age of Reason, if not before then, to the infamous era of the Crusades.

Since the 18th century, European man, in his arrogance, convinced himself that he was the measure of everything, and that his superb rationality would assure him the highest peaks of knowledge, power, and happiness ever achieved in human history. This is quite amazing. Although in this century unspeakable atrocities were committed by this 'rational man'—two savage world wars (including the use of atomic weapons in

---

1. Originally an essay, his concept was later developed into a book:*The End of History and the Last Man*, N.Y., NY, 1993.

2. Samuel Huntington, "The Clash of Civilizations?," *Foreign Affairs* 72/3 (Summer 1993):22-49; the same *Noch ist der Westen Nicht Verloren* (The West is not yet lost), interview with "Die Welt," Hamburg 28:129 June 1997; for other reactions see Ahmet Davotoglu, *The Clash of Interest: An Explanation of World (Dis)order*, "Intellectual Discourse," Istanbul 1994, vol. 2, no. 2, pp. 107–130; Richard Falk, "False Universalism and the Geopolitics of Exclusion: The Case of Islam," *Third World Quarterly*, 1997, vol. 18, no. 1.

the second), the holocaust, Stalinism, and 'ethnic cleansing' in Bosnia—
such bestialities were not enough to shake his conviction. Quite to the
contrary, Western man remains convinced that his civilization is the ultimate one, deserving universal dominance. *His* international law, *his* char-
ter of human rights, *his* economic system, *his* supposedly 'value-free' scientific approach, *his* philosophical epistemology, *his* agnosticism and
atheism are all regarded by him as essential ingredients of an emerging
world culture—'Made in the USA'. In a 'brave new global village' eating
habits, fashion, male and female ideals of beauty, the management of
leisure, sexual mores, architecture, music—you name it—are all to ape
the Western model. What will be left will be the West—and the (insignif-
icant) rest.

And yet, there is an alternative to the Western paradigm, and that is
Islam. True, this religion and its civilization is hardly ever presented by
Western media as a valid alternative that can cope with the world's problems as it enters the 21st century. In fact, Western audiences are bombarded by material presenting Islam as backward, even irrational and
aggressive (if not downright terrorist). To counter these false representations, I isolated 20 major prejudices against Islam and devoted a chapter
to each of them.

When the German version of *Islam: The Alternative*[3] first appeared in
Munich, it caused a media scandal and was soon debated even in the
Bundestag, the German parliament. But no case could be made against
me, and I remained the German ambassador in Rabat until retirement.
However, it became evident that defending Islam after the Salman
Rushdie affair and the second Gulf War was no longer 'politically correct'. When the English translation of *Islam: The Alternative* first
appeared in Great Britain in 1993, some owners even hesitated to display
it in their bookshops.[4] Also—how ironic!—its Arabic version,[5] while
popular in Egypt, the Lebanon, and Syria, encountered a bit of disfavor in
some of the other Muslim countries—perhaps because of its critical
approach to what I consider deviations inside the Muslim world.

Of course, this book was mainly written with the postindustrial and
postmodern Western world in mind where in the coming century, without

---

3. *Der Islam als Alternative*. Eugen Diederichs Verlag, Munich 1992, 2nd edit. 1993,
3rd edit. 1995.
4. Garnet Publishing Ltd., Reading, UK, 1993.
5. *Al Islam ka Badil*. Munich 1993, 2nd edit. Cairo 1997.

a doubt, Islam will become the most vital religion. Not only that; I expect Islam, in the Muslim world itself, to derive major benefits from the experiences and achievements of Muslims in the West, both emigrants and converts. In view of this, American Muslims face three principle tasks (i) to transmit their religion fully intact to the next generation (in a society which is largely permissive and consumerist); (ii) to demonstrate to the American public the spiritual as well as the democratic potential of Islam, showing that this religion is relevant for the solution of most, if not all, of contemporary society's woes, especially as the only effective antidote to drug addiction and to the 'cooling' of interpersonal relations; and finally (iii) to help rejuvenate and refocus the Islamic world at large, particularly through unhampered Islamic scholarship that concentrates on the essentials of our faith, as well as through the transfer of technological and administrative competence from the Occident to the Orient.

Murad Wilfried Hofmann
Istanbul, August 1997

PREFACE TO THE FIRST EDITION

Following the recent tragic events in the Muslim world, bookshops have been flooded by works on the subject of Islam.

On closer examination, however, it becomes clear that only very few authors are willing or indeed able to write about the spiritual background to the cultural phenomenon of 'Islam'. Driven by the fear of radical fundamentalism, 'integrism', a 'Holy War' and the 'Sword of Islam' evoked in a number of titles, many readers are satisfied with superficial sociopolitical commentaries.

But it is impossible to have any understanding, even an idea of the dynamics and the capacity for devotion of contemporary Muslims without a knowledge of their convictions, of the world religion of Islam and its spirituality.

This book, written by a German Muslim, describes the beliefs and civilization of Islam in twenty chapters, each one corresponding to a controversial issue.

It is a scientific plea for Islam, supported by history and conscious of the problems, but free from apologetics.

For as long as the Western world and Communism were opposed to each other, Islam could be regarded as a 'third way', an option between the two philosophies. But today it sees itself as an alternative way of coping with life in a world dualistic once more. Far-sighted observers regard it as almost inevitable that Islam will become the dominant world religion in the twenty-first century, God willing. The reason for this, is suggested in the title of this book. Not only does Islam see itself as the alternative to post-industrial Western society. It is the alternative.

Murad Wilfried Hofmann
Rabat, Ramaḍan 1412 / March, 1992

FOREWORD

"We hate what we do not know." This statement is attributed to 'Ali ibn Abi Talib, fourth Caliph of Islam, first Imām of the Shi'ah, and cousin and son-in-law of the Prophet Muhammad.

Ignorance certainly does breed hatred and fear in relations between humans as well as States, as may be observed throughout history . Today, we find populist publications or TV programs offering to inform the public on little-known subjects; however, this is not the answer and is often times dangerous. The reporter often places too great an emphasis on those points which specifically interest him at the cost of other, equally important facts. A false picture of a culture may thus be painted, triggering what might be termed 'intellectual allergies'.

This is all the more true when it comes to the subject of religion; and Islam typically suffers from misinterpretations of this kind. Just as nineteenth-century artists liked to paint pictures of Muslims (not 'Muhammadans') as savage warriors, with swords in their hands, or in sultry harems, today the word 'Islam' frequently evokes the image of a fanatical bearded oriental scholar, or ruthless terrorist. Images and ideas of this kind are based on misinterpretations which those who have studied Islamic culture or have lived amongst Muslims are in a position to correct.

It is understandable that Islam, a religion born after Christianity, could be regarded as a heresy by medieval European Christians (this is the origin of the old myth that the Prophet Muhammad was a renegade Cardinal!) who saw in this unknown religion similarities to ancient paganism (hence, the strange images of Muhammad depicted in the form of golden icons or statues, found even in the poetry of German Romantics)—an odd distortion of a religion, which has at its center the absolute belief in the unity of God, and whose Prophet, Muhammad (c. 570–632), only described himself as a man to whom revelations were made.

After the death of the Prophet, the rapidly growing Muslim community enjoyed numerous political successes, giving rise to fears amongst

Westerners of the political and military superiority of the Muslims: in the West, they crossed the Straits of Gibraltar in 711, founding the flourishing Andalusian 'Moorish' culture; in the same year they reached Transoxania, laying the foundations for the rich and varied manifestations of Islam in Central Asia; and again in the same year they reached the lower Indus and incorporated the area which now forms Southern Pakistan into the Caliph's Empire.

Spain soon became a relay station between Europe and the Islamic world. To this day numerous scientific, medical, astronomical and cultural terms bear witness to the influence of the sophisticated Muslim culture of Andalusia, where Christians, Jews, and Muslims lived side by side in harmony and mutual influence, the likes of which would never be seen again.

It was in Spain that the first translation of the Qur'an was attempted: this Latin rendering of 1143 remained definitive for centuries and was printed in Basel in 1543 at Luther's suggestion. Until modern times translations of the Holy Book have always been accompanied by translators' apologia. Of course, the Qur'an, revealed between 610 and 622 in Makkah and then Madinah, poses almost insurmountable problems for the translator. For the Muslim it is the word of God, revealed in clear Arabic, and its translation can only be superficial, for who can render the unsurpassable beauty of the Word of God in another language? The many subtleties and overtones which accompany every Arabic word in the Qur'an make any translation from the Arabic extremely difficult. No translation can reproduce the spirit as well as the written form, and this itself leads to difficulties in understanding it. In addition, the arrangement of the Qur'an compounds the difficulty for the non-Muslim. (The present arrangement dates back to the third Caliph, 'Uthman.) The 114 chapters (*surahs*) are not arranged chronologically, but generally in decreasing order of length. Beginning with the opening chapter, the *Fātiḥah*, (an opening prayer), the Qur'an progresses from the largest chapters to the smallest ones, and concludes with two chapters for 'seeking refuge with God'. But, because the short surahs belong to the earliest period of the preaching while the long ones frequently come from the later period (when Muhammad was concerned with the establishment of the community in Madinah), it is not easy for the new reader to find his way through the Holy Book. There is a danger that sentences may be read out of context, leading to false conclusions.

The non-Muslim is scarcely aware of the extent to which the Qur'an permeates the Islamic languages, that it has given them the Arabic alphabet, or how far it has influenced their verbal imagery. For the most part, the Islamic sciences grew out of the study of the Qur'an and the arts, such as calligraphy and modulating recitation, developed in order to give the Word of God worthy form. Classical works in the languages of the Islamic world—whether they be in Arabic, Persian, Turkish, Urdu, or any other language spoken by Muslims—can hardly be understood without a thorough knowledge of the Qur'anic vocabulary.

For the Muslim, the Qur'an is the Word of God 'made book,' just as for the Christian, Christ is the Word of God 'made flesh'. Muhammad is the vessel into which this word was transmitted to the world; and just as the Qur'an has been misunderstood for centuries, the figure of Muhammad has also been misinterpreted. For the Muslim faithful, he represents the shining, ideal example for every situation in life—his sunnah (his conduct) is the accepted model. But the fact that Muhammad was a prophet and teacher who did not withdraw from the world, but was a man with a family (the marriages he concluded in his later years were disliked particularly by the ascetic medieval Christian Church) and that, in the years following his emigration (*hijrah*) from Makkah to Madinah in 622, he organized a State, seemed irreconcilable with the ideal of a holy man. But for the Muslim this very duality, the combination of religion and worldly activity, is the sign of a true religious leader (hence, the endless discussions on the nature of an 'Islamic' State).

And just as over the centuries the Qur'an has again and again been and is still being interpreted afresh by scholars, mystics, and devotees, more and more legends have been woven around the figure of Muhammad. The man who always emphasized his mere humanity (in mystical interpretations) has been likened to a shining light, the first being created by God, the real purpose and aim of creation, and (in modern secular interpretations) an ideal social reformer.

Historically and geographically, Islam is extraordinarily wide-ranging; however, the many local variations of Islam—in Indonesia, for example, or Black Africa—should not surprise us. After all, there are also many different forms of Christianity, ranging from the colorful iconostasis of the Greek Orthodox Church to the bare House of God of the Calvinists, from Irish Catholicism to the strictness of the Methodists.

Despite the variations in the local colorings of Islam, the common basis is one and the same: the creed that God is One, without companions, uncreated, reigning from eternity to eternity and that Muhammad is His Messenger. The first half of the Islamic creed is "There is no divinity except God". The worst sin is to suggest that he had a companion. The second half of the creed attests to the fact that "Muhammad is God's Messenger". This means that he, the last in a long line of Prophets that began with Adam, transmitted God's final revelation, once again clearly delivering God's eternal law.

We must bear these simple facts in mind, never forgetting that Islam, whose name means 'submission to God,' places God and his Word at the center of life. Many of the misunderstandings we encounter today arise from our tendency to view everything from the perspective of the ideals of late twentieth-century Western society. This is where the real difficulty lies: can we accept values of a pretty much 'godless' society as absolute? Our grandmothers' generation would probably have been shocked by many things that we now regard as normal, permissible aspects of everyday life. Do we, for example, still go to church with heads covered, as we once did? Covering the hair is an ancient tradition; according to early beliefs, hair is endowed with great power. (We all know the story of Samson, who lost his strength when his locks were cut off.) Since the earliest times Jewish societies covered the head. The devout Jewess covers her hair, and the devout Jewish male student or professor even attends lectures at Harvard with his Yarmulka or skull cap—why then should a Turkish girl not wear a headscarf? The Islamic religion, however, requires a head-covering *only* during periods of prayer or Qur'anic teaching, and not at any other time.[1] Women and men alike are called to perform all religious duties, and the Qur'an constantly refers to 'devout Muslim men *and* women'.

"We hate what we do not know," but when we trace the roots of a foreign culture much is clarified. We learn, for example, that the frequently employed term 'holy war' is an expression which stems from the Christian language of the crusades; the Arabic term, jihad, means 'to strive, to endeavor'—the believer should 'strive along the path of God,' i.e., defend his belief and, when necessary, help spread the religion. In addition, jihad refers to an inner struggle against one's own weaknesses.

---

1. This view does not correspond to orthodox Islamic doctrine; see pp. 125-128 below.

We could go through the time-consuming process of examining a long
list of similar misunderstandings; therefore, let us be grateful that in this
work a German Muslim, trained in law and philosophy, offers the reader
his own interpretations. To a great extent Dr. Hofmann's analysis of the
ideal Sunni Islam coincides with the teachings of the late Pakistani scholar Fazlur Rahman who was persecuted by the ultra-orthodox scholars of
Pakistan for preaching 'the living Sunnah'. He focused on the spirit of the
Prophet's example, and his analyses (which also included a rejection of
Ibn 'Arabi's mysticism) were of major importance. Dr. Hofmann also
found a similar concern for a reinterpretation of Islam on the basis of the
Qur'an in the Indo-Muslim poet-philosopher Iqbal. He emphasized the
idea of the Qur'an being inexhaustible in all its facets, but also taught of
man's duties to improve his world and develop his God-given talents.
This includes the rejection of what is often referred to as Islamic fatalism,
an attitude regarded by many to be the cause of Islam's stagnation. Dr
Hofmann's comments on this subject seem to be particularly important.
An absolute trust in God, which is a feature of Islam, does not exclude the
possibility of human striving; rather, it helps the devout Muslim to bear
whatever fate comes to him—he trusts that God knows what is best for
him at any one point in time. The Prophet said, "This world is the field
(that yields its fruits) for the next (world)." Every action carries within it
its own fruit. Islamic fatalism does not prevent Muslims from acting;
rather, it teaches that every event, even suffering, has a meaning. Anyone
who has seen a devout Turkish mother receive news of the death of her
tenth and last son, and still be in a position to console her weeping
friends, will know what I mean.

Of course, for modern Western society this kind of attitude is alien,
even incomprehensible, despite the fact that it is very close to early
Christianity: it is an attitude of complete trust in God, whose names
include the Creator, the Preserver, and the Judge, and whose most frequently used names are the Beneficent and the Merciful (every surah of
the Qur'an and every activity begins with the phrase "In the name of God,
the Beneficent, the Merciful").

The tendency to identify contemporary Islam with terrorism or fundamentalism (again, a term taken from the American history of religion) is
tragic, although to some extent understandable, since it is those manifestations of another religion which are most alien to our own understanding
of religion which always attract the most attention, and because moderate

groups never have a high profile. But do we identify Christianity with terrorism every time we hear of attacks in various European countries? It
sometimes seems to me that the fear of the Turks, who were able to reach
Vienna on two occasions—in 1529 and 1683—still lives on beneath the
surface in central Europe, coloring many people's view of the religion of
the Turks and Arabs, Persians and Muslims in the Indo-Indonesian world.
Even educated people know little of the rich treasures of Islamic literature and art, and seldom realize that the Alhambra in Granada or the much
praised Taj Mahal in India are the works of Muslim architects. And how
many people know that Islam honors Jesus and his Virgin Mother? The
Muslim regards Jesus as the last Prophet sent by God before Muhammad,
as a man who preached love of God and asceticism. However, he believes
that Jesus was not crucified, rather, that he was raised up to Heaven.

In this book, the reader will find many new or for him unknown interpretations. At times he may be amazed, if not shocked by the author's
sharply defined position, which is based firmly on classical Islam and
which does not prize the Islamic mysticism which is more kindred to
many Westerners. The reader will find Islam, which many Westerners see
as a relic of outdated medieval forms, presented as a religion very much
alive and worth living, and, we hope, will gain a deeper understanding of
this faith.

Finally, we should not forget Goethe's dictum to be found in his *West-
Eastern Divan,* a work which testifies to his great insight into the spiritual world of Islam:

If Islam means submission to God's Will
Then in Islam we all live and die.

Annemarie Schimmel
Advent 1991

ISLAM AND THE WEST

Towards the end of his life the Prophet of Islam (peace be upon him) sent messages to surrounding rulers, such as the Negus of Abyssinia, Khosrow II of Persia (590–628) and the Eastern Roman Emperor Heraclius (610–641). Muhammad called upon them in simple and unambiguous terms to accept Islam for their own benefit and the benefit of their peoples.[1]

This episode in diplomatic history marks the beginning of relations between Islam and the West—never broken off, nor ever relaxed, for 1400 years—relations which, despite many fruitful economic and intellectual contacts, have always been confrontational.

It is for this reason, against the background of the historical Christian–Islamic conflict, that today West and East, Occident and Orient are usually regarded not as complementary but conflicting, even hostile worlds, facing each other fearfully and without comprehension. The collective memory of both parties is wide awake.

The course of history, particularly the speed and extent of early Islamic expansion, explains a great deal: hardly had Muhammad died (632) before Syria and Palestine (634–35), Persia (637), Egypt (643–649), Armenia (652), Cyprus (653), the Maghrib (670) and even Spain (711) became Islamic. Constantinople suffered its first siege as early as 688. On this occasion, in the figure of Abu Ayub al Ansari, the flag-bearer, one of the Prophet's companions was still present.

In view of successes like these it is understandable that the West should cling to the notion that Islam is an aggressive religion that owes its expansion to 'the fire and the sword'. It is true that from a military point of view the surrounding Christian and Iranian areas were unable to oppose the fearless religious fervor of the early Muslims. But it is also true that the

---

1. See Ibn Isḥāq/Ibn Hishām, *The Life of Muhammad*, translated by A. Guillaume, Oxford 1955, pp. 652ff. The message to Heraclius transmitted by Dihya b. Khalifa al Kalbi al Khazraji was explained to the Emperor at his request by Abu Sufyan. See hadith no. 4553 in *Ṣaḥīḥ al Bukhārī*, translated into German by Muh. Rassoul, Cologne 1989, pp. 436-438, and into English by Muhammad Muhsin Khan, *Ṣaḥīḥ al Bukhārī*, vol. VI, Chicago, IL, 1979, hadith no. 60175 (*Tafsīr al Qur'an*).

small number of early Muslim warriors would have been unable to conquer such large areas, had the population not joined them en masse.

Certainly, one of the reasons for this is not exactly flattering to the West: heterodox Christians in the Maghrib and Mashriq—including Arians and Donatists—accepted Islamic rule easily because they too did not believe in either the divine nature of Jesus nor the Trinity.[2] In the eleventh century, Islam spread to Senegal, Mali, Ghana and Chad without the aid of either fire or sword and is still spreading peacefully throughout Africa today.

The world-shattering dynamism of the Muslims deeply affected the scientific and cultural worlds of the time. They achieved epoch-making results in all areas of the arts and sciences—including mathematics, optics, botany, surgery, ophthalmology, hygiene, lexicography, history, sociology—and in the continuation of Aristotelian philosophy, which had been forgotten in the West. In these and other areas, Islamic civilization outshone Western civilization from the ninth to the fourteenth centuries, even if we only take into account the likes of al Razi (Rhazes), al Biruni, Ibn Rushd (Averroës), Ibn Sina (Avicenna), Ibn Khaldun, Ibn Baṭṭutah and al Khwarizmi.[3] When the Muslims were finally halted, as in France in 733, the Western world launched its counter-attack with crusades (eleventh to thirteenth centuries) and the Portuguese–Spanish Reconquista. (The Byzantine Christians soon learned the meaning of Christian 'fire and sword' with the Latins' (or "Franks'") sacking of Constantinople in 1204.) And then it was again the West's turn to be afraid, following the Ottomans' capture of Constantinople (1453) and the advance of their armies through the Balkans as far as Vienna (1529 and 1683).

Since the eighteenth century it seemed as though these epic conflicts gradually would come to an end. From that time until the present the two worlds drifted apart in a dramatic manner. Since the Renaissance and the Enlightenment, the West has undergone an almost explosive scientific and technological development, giving rise to an enormous economic and

---

2. At his first encounter with Muslims in 614, the Negus of Abyssinia saw no contradiction between his and their comprehension of Jesus and Mary; see Ibn Isḥāq, *op. cit.*, pp. 146ff; Martin Lings, *Muhammad*, New York 1983, pp. 81ff.

3. Since Sigrid Hunke's bestseller *Allahs Sonne über dem Abendland* (Stuttgart, 1960) these facts should be common knowledge; see also *Das Vermächtnis des Islams*, 2 vols, Munich 1983; Muh. Hamidullah, *Introduction to Islam*, 5th edition, Luton 1980, pp. 443–477; *The Legacy of Muslim Spain*, ed. Salma Khadra Jayyusi, Leiden, 1992.

military dynamism unmatched in the rest of the world, and which is still seen as proof of a general superiority of the Christian civilization.

At the same time, the Islamic world declined into a state of such incompetence, lethargy, and decadence that colonization by the imperialistic Western powers of the nineteenth century was inevitable. In 1924, it was not unrealistic to believe that Atatürk had dealt Islam its death blow with the abolition of the Caliphate.

Thus, from the middle of this century onwards, it seemed only a matter of time before Western culture would become the 'obligatory example' (Theodore von Laue), the world culture, implying the westernization of all other cultures. From Seoul to Soho future people world-wide would wear jeans, eat hamburgers, drink Coca Cola, smoke Marlboro, speak English, watch CNN, live in a Bauhaus style house in a democratic State and probably be *pro forma* members of some Christian Church.

Today, the causes of the demise of the Islamic world are still under discussion.[4] In my opinion there are three main contributing factors.

First, in the thirteenth century the Christian world and the Mongols, almost simultaneously, 'put the screws on' Islam, militarily speaking, hitting a major nerve as both centers of Islamic intellectual culture were overrun—Cordoba in 1236, Baghdad in 1258. To this day the Islamic world has not recovered from these catastrophes.

Second, in the fourteenth century the idea became fixed in Islamic jurisprudence and soon after within the general community, that everything worth knowing had already been known and was better understood by earlier generations closer to the source. This led to scholarship being based on imitation (*taqlid*), a general un-Islamic stagnation in intellectual life and a neglect of natural sciences (see also the chapter "Religion and Knowledge").

Third, the last and by far the most important factor is to be found not within the Islamic world but within the Western world: it cannot be denied that its huge material boom from the nineteenth century onwards was inextricably linked to a gradual break with the Christian faith. Indeed, the motivating force behind the scientifically and economically successful scientism and positivism of this 'century without God'[5] was a world-centered attitude, if not always atheism, then an agnosticism of

---

4. See Peter Waltner,'Warum ist die islamische Welt unterentwickelt?', *CIBEDO*, Frankfurt 1988, no. 6, pp. 161–173; Marshall G. Hodgson, *The Venture of Islam*, vol. III, Chicago, 1974, p. 238.

5. The title of a book by Alfred Müller-Armack which appeared in 1948.

which Feuerbach, Marx, Darwin, Nietzsche and Freud were the apostles. Since then, scientific rationalism, which only admits the validity of quantifiable sensory perception, has become the dominant Occidental ideology of efficiency. Belief in God is perhaps tolerated as a probability theory à la Swinburn,[6] but anything to do with ultimate issues becomes taboo, thanks to a 'magic of death repression' (W. Freund).

In the twentieth century even the masses carry these ideas. As a result of the subjectivism and relativism they have acquired, they live a vulgar *de facto* atheism whose idols are power, money, beauty, popularity and sex. It was accepted that science, as opposed to the religion it had repressed, was incompetent for determining the meaning of life, yet it was thought that this issue would simply disappear together with the irrational Christian beliefs that had fathered it.[7]

This loss of transcendence, this vulgar materialism found in both the East and the West, has led to the greedy hedonism of a people without constraints, who see their emotions as the measure of all things and who expect unending 'progress' to lead to a consumer paradise on earth.[8] This is where even "post-modern" industrial society is heading, a society whose highest principles continue to be of economic nature: growth, efficiency, full employment, profit maximization, specialization.

Alfred Müller-Armack described this logical process in his book *Religion und Wirtschaft* (Religion and Economy, 1959) in even fewer words:

> Because man has paid for his freedom to deny God with the compulsion to populate his world with idols and demons, the history of faith . . . is incomplete without the history of the lack of faith. God as the highest value is replaced by idols which . . . lead to a progressive loss of substance. The history of the perversion of faith, of pseudo-religion, is the history of destructive forces which lead to catastrophes. (p. xv)

Neither Islam, nor any other culture possessing a religious nature, could withstand the material power generated by an onslaught motivated in this

---

6. Richard Swinburn, *The Existence of God*, Oxford 1979.

7. In the words of Hans Oesterle, *Frankfurter Allgemeine Zeitung,* 9 September 1987.

8. Described in greater detail by, amongst others, René Guénon, *Crisis of the Modern World,* 1981; Guénon, *The Reign of Quantity and the Signs of the Times,* 1983; see also Vance Packard, *The Sexual Wilderness,* 1968, and Charles A. Reich, *The Greening of America,* 1971.

hedonist way. For this reason—as regards the third main reason for Islamic 'backwardness'—it is erroneous to ask what has 'gone wrong' recently with the Muslim world; for, in fact, it is the Western world which has gone wrong![9]

Then, in the 1960s and 1970s, contrary to what one had grown to expect, *both* sides underwent momentous breaks in development. But Islam, though wracked with crises, was not buried. On the contrary, it has become reanimated to such an extent that ancient fears of Islam have been revived. And in contrast, crisis now looms in the Western industrial society.

This was unexpected at the time but today both developments are seen as inevitable.

Sociologists such as Daniel Bell (Harvard) have observed that the economic success of the capitalist world undermines the very values (and, therefore, the behavior) of the Max Weber-like Protestant ethic on which it is based. This self-destructive mechanism can be observed in the fact that in affluent societies virtues such as diligence, thrift, discipline, patience, brotherliness and courage are defamed and perverted so as to become negative qualities, or are replaced with new values and new codes of conduct, which are really 'post-industrial' to the extent that— generally practiced—they could not sustain an industrial society.[10]

Thus, individualism is perverted to narcissism, brotherliness to the para-rational collective behavior of groupies at rock concerts, self-determination ("My belly belongs to me") to moral anarchy, liberality to libertinage, tolerance to value-neutrality, competition to consumer madness, equality to leveling (instead of equal chances, equal results), sensitivity to whining, being careful to a refusal to take risks, respect to fear, eroticism to sexual athletics, diligence to workaholism, and flexibility to contempt for tradition. In short, as Marcel Boisot established in 1984, such perversions are inevitable when the key factors of rationality, freedom, and love are no longer held in balance. This is easily worked through: rationality without freedom leads to the 'Gulag Archipelago' and rationality without

---

9. This is why Muslims react so bitterly to the Orientalists' suggestion that Islam should finally make up its own 'Renaissance' and 'Enlightenment,' as if Islam had missed its train or should also slide down a slippery slope.

10. Daniel Bell, *The Cultural Contradictions of Capitalism,* London 1976; see also Wolfgang Slim Freund, "Überlegungen zur Dialektik zwischen 'Rationalität' und 'magischem Denken' in westlichen Industriegesellschaften," in *Osterreichische Zeitschrift für Soziologie,* 1986, no. 3, pp. 47 ff.

love to Auschwitz; freedom without love leads to the exploitation of others, freedom without rationality to self-destruction.[11]

The modern scene in all industrial States shows symptoms of dysfunction, symbolized by the 'green' dropout searching for alternatives to the very system which gave him wealth and freedom. Young people like this are manifesting something very fundamental through their specific problems, obsessions, or 'hang-ups': pervasive fear, the need for emotional security, malaise towards the secret compulsions of hypertrophic technology, resistance to 'consumer terror,' and rejection of the idolization of unmitigated rationality, whether in the economy or in nuclear deterrence.

In fact, they are demonstrating that one cannot take away man's transcendental links without subjecting him to a meaningless, boundless cultural 'freedom of the damned'.

Let us look at them, these victims of a seemingly value-agnostic society. They have everything—autonomy, protection from the cradle to the grave, sex without taboos, drugs on demand, a great deal of free time, lots of cash, and every human right imaginable. But what they feel is an existential emptiness, what they long for is warmth in society and a guru who radiates authority. And behind all this is an increasingly urgent quest for *meaning*.

This is the background to the sudden reappearance of religiosity as "a psycho boom with many sects and their extremely subjective contemplation of their navels" (Rosemarie Stein), which causes even established Churches to reflect upon their mystical potential. This trend toward the esoteric, toward the 'Jesus trip,' may follow strange paths. Sooner or later, as search for an alternative, for a valid religion, it encounters the phenomenon of Islam which is in the ascendant, and which is now understood as the third way between the utopia of Western and Eastern materialism.[12]

The corresponding development in the Islamic world began with the independence movements of this century that finally led to its political self-determination. (With Algeria [1962] being the last colonized Muslim state, except for Palestine, to regain its sovereignty.) Initially these young States and their heroes—Muhammad Ali Jinna, Gamal Abd al Nasser,

---

11. Marcel Boisot, "Eine moralische Waffe—Das westliche Wertesystem," in *Journal of the European Institute for Security* 3/84, Luxemburg; for similar views from a Muslim perspective see Abdel-Wahab Elmessiri, "The Crisis of Modernity and Other Common Ground," *Al Ahram Weekly*, 12-23 July, 1997, p. 7.

12. For details see *Religion in Contemporary Europe*, ed. John Fulton and Peter Gee, Lewiston, NY, 1994; and *Islam, Globalization and Postmodernity*, ed. Akbar S. Ahmed and Hastings Donnan, N.Y., NY, 1994.

Habib Bourgiba, Ahmed Ben Bella, Houari Boumedienne—sought to copy Western models: liberalism, nationalism, socialism, communism. Islam played no specific or prominent role, since early Arabism was as unreligious as early Zionism. The Algerian FLN and the Tunisian Neo-Destour were secular at leadership level. This assimilation of the West, which continued after independence, corresponded at heart to the Kemalist doctrine and the ideals of westernized, modernistic Muslims, such as Muhammad Arkoun in France and Bassam Tibi in Germany.[13]

But all of these experiments failed due to the inability to cope with population growth, low exports, flight of capital, nepotism, corruption, debt, and the emigration of intellectuals, despite the fact that many attempts were made to solve problems together through the Arab League (1944), the Organization of the Islamic Conference (OIC) (1969), the Gulf Cooperation Council (GCC) (1981) and the Union of the Maghrib States (UMA) (1989).

Against this background, at the beginning of the 1970s the phenomenon of re-Islamization arose, and has been relentlessly analyzed ever since, with its aspects of Islamism (*Islāmīyah*), fundamentalism and integrism, to which chapters of this book are dedicated.[14]

Initially, it was believed and hoped that re-Islamization was but a social protest movement. Seeing the revival of Islam simply as a function of the technological gap only proved that the analysts were unable to comprehend the religious factor. Clearly, they lacked an understanding of people who take their religion seriously, even in cases where the Islamic world was regarded benevolently through the eyes of third world romanticism (*tiers mondisme*).

Meanwhile, Bassam Tibi had shown that the term 're-Islamization' contained a false premise, because, except amongst some Western-oriented urban 'intellectuals,' Islam had never lost its significance anywhere as a belief and reference system, not even in Turkey, but had retained its relevance under a "thin veneer of modernization" (Arnold Hottinger).

Today, it is agreed that the renewed manifestation of Islam must be seen as the re-entry of the sacred into the public domain. (Gilles Kepel empha-

---

13. See Martin Kramer, *Arab Awakening and Islamic Revival*, New Burnswick, NJ., 1996.

14. See Bassam Tibi, *Die Krise des modernen Islam*, Munich 1981; Wolfgang Slim Freund, reviewed in: *Islam und der Westen*, 1982, no. 3, p. 12, Freund, "Jüdischer und islamischer Fundamentalismus" in: *Orient* 1987, no. 2, pp. 216 ff.; Detlef Khalid, "Die Entwicklungen im Islam," *Neue Zürcher Zeitung*, 28 April 1983; Peter Scholl-Latour, *Allah ist mit den Standhaften*, Stuttgart 1983; Wilhelm Dietl, *Heiliger Krieg für Allah*, Munich 1983; *The Islamist Dilemma—The Political Role of Islamist Movements in the Contemporary Arab World*, ed. Laura Guazzone, Reading, U.K., 1995.

sizes this in the title of his book *La revanche d'Allah*.) Logically, this translates into a fundamental rejection of Western secularism. The Islamic world regards the Western loss of, and break with, the transcendental as a mutilation of human faculties, reacting to it with a counter-project which does not herald the end of modernism as such but Eurocentrism. (After the demise of Communism the world is once again a bi-polar one, as far as the history of ideas is concerned.)

The revival of Islam also offers the traumatized Muslim of the Third World a chance to retrace his roots and to regain his sense of dignity by withdrawing from competition (which cannot be won anyway) with the West in the consumer sector. The apparently endless chain of humiliations of the Arab world, especially in Palestine, has prepared the political ground for a religious and moral revolt.

Of course there are 'Islamistic' forces in the Islamic world too, who use religion primarily to motivate and justify their political aim of changing the status quo, 'Islamic' terrorists being among them. In the context of the revolutionary Shi'ah seizure of power in Iran (1979) and the Gulf War (1990–91), such Muslims behaved in a manner "which damaged Islam more than anything else this century" (Wolfgang Günter Lerch).[15]

Indeed, as so often in their history, Occident and Orient once again are witnessing a scene of destruction. During the Gulf War, fear spread amongst Muslims in Europe and the USA, just as amongst Europeans in the Maghrib and the Near East. It seemed as if we were all waiting for new crusades, in both directions. There was no more talk of a Christian–Islamic dialogue (see the chapter "The Islamic View of Christianity"); Islam was more demonized than it had been for a long time.[16]

From this sad 1400-year history of the relations between Islam and the West we may draw the lesson that both worlds, especially in the era of weapons of mass destruction, must approach each other with tolerance if world peace is to be maintained and the predicted "clash of civilizations" (S. Huntington) to be avoided. The better the West understands Islam and Islam the West, the easier this will be. This book attempts to break through the "total, culturally determined barriers to understanding" between the two (Wolfgang Slim Freund) that are standing in the way of mutual comprehension.

---

15. *Frankfurter Allgemeine Zeitung*, 16 October 1986, p. 9.

16. Sigrid Hunke's *Allah ist ganz anders: Enthüllungen von 1001 Vorurteilen über die Araber*, Bad König, 1990 was unable to counter this trend in spite of uncovering "1001 prejudices."

THE COMPLETE FAITH

Christian missionaries attribute the rapid penetration of Islam into West Africa, Senegal, Cameroon, and the Ivory Coast to the simplicity of its teachings and its freedom from complicated mysteries. If this is true, it must be possible to describe this religion in a single chapter.

To be a Muslim rests on two assumptions, (a) the belief in a personal (but genderless), transcendental God (but who is active in the world);[1] and (b) the belief in His revelations, ultimately leading from Abraham to Muhammad.

Muslims *believe* in God because His existence is logical to them in view of the existence of the world (i.e., ontologically) and its contingency (i.e., causally), despite their knowledge that, from a scientific point of view, it is questionable to infer what cannot be perceived by the senses from what can, especially since the validity of our logic for such operations is not verifiable.

In the first part of the two-part Islamic profession of faith the Muslim professes his faith in God (*ashhadu*), though not in the simplest possible form (*ashhadu an lā ilāha illa Allāh*) but, following *Sūrat al Ikhlāṣ* (112), he declares his opposition to dualistic, trinitarian or polytheistic ideas of God.

> **Say: He, God, is the One God:**
> **God the Eternal, the Uncaused Cause of All Being**
> **He begets not nor is he begotten;**
> **and there is nothing that could be compared with Him.** [2]

With the formulation "I profess that there is no God besides God" (*ashhadu an lā ilāha illa Allāh*) the Muslim emphasizes the unity and uniqueness of God. From a Muslim point of view, the principle of unity (*tawḥīd*) applies to spirit and matter, soul and body, science and religion, man and

---

1. That God is "closer to us than our jugular vein" (50:16) should not be understood in terms of pantheism. See the Throne Verse, *Ayat al Kursi*, (2:255) for a dialectical description of both the immanence *and* transcendence of Allah.
2. Translation by Muhammad Asad, *The Message of the Qur'an*, Gibraltar, 1980.

nature and also to Muslims as social beings: their aim is always to unite as a community (*Ummah*).

As radical theists Muslims are agnostics in terms of epistemological theory, regarding God's being, His essence, and His actions. They believe that it is only possible to define Him in negative terms; for example, that God has no beginning and no end, and therefore, cannot not be. Muslims are also convinced that it is impossible to find the way of life most fitting for human beings merely from the contemplation of nature. (The history of the theories and systems of "natural law" proves them right.) This is why they insist on the indispensability of revelation.

Furthermore, they *believe* that God sent His guidance to human beings through prophets of monotheism like Abraham, Moses and Jesus, whose messages were 'sealed' by the Qur'an, the culminating message brought by Muhammad ("Muhammad is . . . the seal of the prophets" [33:40], i.e., the last one). This is why the second part of the Islamic profession of faith necessarily says "and I profess that Muhammad is His messenger" (*wa ashhadu anna Muhammadan rasūlu Allah*).

Only that which is finished, in the case of divine revelation that which is complete, is to be sealed. Despite the work of Moses and Jesus there was a need and opportunity for completion: a *need,* because, from an Islamic point of view, Jews and Christians had falsified the message passed on to them—the Jews, through the postulation of a 'chosen' people negotiating with God; the Christians, through the postulation of a son conceived as God; an *opportunity,* because human development in the seventh century had progressed to the point where earlier norms could be replaced by definitive new ones.[3]

This explains the verse revealed on the ninth day of the month of Dhu al Ḥijjah, the Day of 'Arafah during Muhammad's final pilgrimage in 632, which was 81 or 82 days before Muhammad's death:

---

3. The possibility of replacing earlier verses by later ones, alluded to in 2:106, is generally believed not to refer to metaphysical or historical facts. I agree with Muhammad Asad that *ayah* is to be read here as 'message.' The implication is that there can be abrogation only in relation to pre-Qur'anic revelations. See Muhammad Asad, *The Message of the Qur'an*, Gibraltar 1980, footnote 87 to 2:106; and Mahmoud Ayoub, *The Qur'an and Its Interpreters*, vol. 1, Albany 1984, p. 138. Wherever there are conflicting rules within the Qur'an, they must be seen in a relationship of *lex specialis* and *lex generalis*, the former overriding the latter, even if revealed at a later date. On the subject of the gradual prohibition of alcohol, see Helmut Gätje, *Koran und Koranexegese*, Zurich, 1971, pp. 264 ff.

> **This day have I perfected your religion for you and completed My favor on you and chosen for you Islam (i.e., submission to Allah) as your religion. (5:3)[4]**

'Muslim' is the active participle of the verbs *salama* or *aslama,* which correspond to the 'slm' root in Arabic (Arabic words being made up of three-letter roots), and which express the idea of intactness and submission. Accordingly, in the original Qur'anic definition, a Muslim is one who finds salvation through voluntary submission. On this basis Jesuit Father Johannes Sokolowsky SJ provided an exemplary definition of 'Islam' as "The submission (to God) which brings peace, and causes one to be fully in harmony, healthy and spiritually normal."[5] This is why men like Abraham, Jesus, and some pre-Islamic Arab hermits may be regarded as Muslims.

Today, however, 'Muslim' describes someone who finds peace in submission to God specifically in accordance with the Qur'an and the Prophet's model behavior (Sunnah); this includes earlier revelations as much as they are authentic and remain valid.

Thus, for example, a Muslim follows the Ten Commandments of the Old Testament and the commandment to love thy neighbor of the New Testament. For him, as for Jews and Christians who have maintained their belief, there are six articles of faith which, according to the Qur'an, are the basis of all theological understanding of cosmic reality (2:285; 4:136; 9:51):

- the existence of God;
- the existence of other spiritual beings ("His angels");
- the existence of divine revelation ("His books");
- the sending of prophets ("His Messengers");
- Final Judgment / Life after death;
- predestination (see the chapter "Fatalism").

On the other hand, Islam prescribes a code of conduct and worship which is specific to it alone, and which, together with the profession of faith (*shahādah*), comprises the so-called 'five pillars':

- ritual prayer at fixed times, five times a day (salah),

---

4. Translation by Yusuf Ali, *The Meaning of the Holy Qur'an,* New Edition with revised translation, commentary and newly compiled subject index, amana publications, Beltsville, Md, 1996.

5. 'Friede und Islam,' in *Geist und Leben,* 1983, no. 2, p. 145.

• the annual payment of a capital tax (zakah),
• fasting during the day throughout the month of Ramaḍān (ṣawm),
• as far as possible, a pilgrimage to Makkah (ḥajj).[6]

These pillars show that Islam is based on belief and deed, prayer and work; even spiritual activities such as prayer are linked to physical activities. This is clearly expressed in *Sūrat al 'Aṣr* revealed in Makkah:

Surely man is in continuous loss, except those who believe and do good deeds and urge one another to act rightfully and urge one another to exercise patience. (103:1-3)[7]

This is a miniature portrait of the good Muslim; he prays and trusts in God, does good works for his neighbors as well as for Islam, without activism or arrogance.

A Muslim may sin without calling into question whether he is a Muslim. But if he stops praying and, therefore, interrupts his contact with God, he can hardly be considered a Muslim. This prayer, in its ritually prescribed form (salah), is not a prayer of request but a prayer of praise, which does not, of course, exclude other forms and contents of prayer.

As the final revelation, the Qur'an is the most important, though not the only, basis of Islam. This book, with its 6236 verses (*ayāt*) unsystematically distributed over 114 *sūrahs* (parts or chapters), mostly in rhyming prose, contains the revelations which Muhammad received between about 610 and 632 in their complete and original form. For the Muslim, the Qur'an is the Word of God, not created but revealed in historical times and in the Arabic language: the only miracle of Islam (and at the same time Muhammad's 'miracle of attestation').[8] Thus, the Qur'an is not—as most of the Old and New Testament are—'inspired,' second-hand narration, but it is God's speech throughout, either in the first person singular or plural, or in the third person singular (so that we always remain conscious of the inadmissibility of personalizing His being anthropomorphically).

---

6. 4:136; 2:285.

7. Translation by Rashid Said Kassab, *Translation of the Meanings of the Glorious Qur'an*, Amman, 1994.

8. For the history of the Qur'an see Ahmad von Denffer, *'Ulūm al Qur'an, An Introduction to the Sciences of the Qur'an*, Leicester 1983; and also Mohamed Talbi, *Reflexions sur le Coran*, Paris 1989; Paul Schwarzenau, *Korankunde für Christen*, 2nd edition, Hamburg 1990. For the orientalist's point of view: Rudi Paret, *Muhammad und der Koran*, Stuttgart, 1985.

A non-Muslim may deny the authenticity of the revelation, but he cannot deny the authenticity of the text. This was established by Western orientalists who had set out to prove the very opposite, using the same critical methods that had invalidated all but fragments of the Bible, in particular, the New Testament.

A non-Muslim may reject the content of the Qur'an, but he cannot ignore the fascination which emanates from the power of the language and the poetic force of the text, which enthralled Johann Wolfgang von Goethe and Friedrich Rückert.[9] For Arabs the extraordinary purity and harmony of the language of the Qur'an is proof of its supernatural origin. Unfortunately, some Muslims also extrapolate from God's statement in the Qur'an: "**We have not neglected a single thing in the book**" (6:38) that the Qur'an has an encyclopedic competence in areas that have nothing to do with theology and ethics, in particular, scientific phenomena.

That Maurice Bucaille has shown that, compared to the other Holy Books, only the Qur'an is not in conflict with modern scientific knowledge, is quite a different aspect.[10] Personally, I find the reference in *Sūrat al 'Alaq* (96), *ayah* 2 to the fertilization process in woman most impressive: from a medical point of view it was described correctly in the Qur'an 1400 years ago as a clinging or lodging (of the sperm cell). Until very recently the Arabic word in question, *'alaq*, was mistranslated simply because in this context no one could imagine anything appropriate for this word.

Although it is not possible to translate the Qur'an without loss of meaning, not least because of the particular characteristics of the Arabic language, in which it is possible to make temporally indeterminate statements, and because of its richness of associations, it has in fact become the most frequently translated,[11] most printed book in the history of the

9. Ahmad von Denffer, 'Der Islam und Goethe,' *Al Islām,* Munich 1990-1994. Achmed Schmiede, 'Goethe und der Islam', *Al Islam,* 1982, no. 6, p. 15; The German Orientalist poet Friedrich Rückert translated the Qur'an primarily in verse form and very well (*Der Koran* 1888, reprint Hildesheim 1980). Rather puzzlingly, Kant's doctorate certificate of 1755 shows the *basmalah* hand written on it: *"bi ism Allah al Rahmān al Rahīm"*; see Ahmad von Denffer, 'Deutsche Denker und der Islam', *Al Islam* 1985, no. 2, p. 20.

10. Maurice Bucaille, *The Bible, the Qur'an and Science: the Holy Scriptures examined in the light of modern knowledge,* translated by Alastair D. Pannell and Maurice Bucaille, Indianapolis 1978

11. See the *World Bibliography of Translations of the Meanings of the Holy Qur'an, Printed Translations 1515–1980,* IRCICA, Instanbul, 1986. As the first complete translation into English it lists a version dated 1648, based on the 1647 French translation by the Sieur du Ryer. The first translation into German was made in 1616 by Salomon Schweiggem based on the Italian.

world, and the only book which hundreds of thousands of people know by heart. It is *its* Arabic which now holds the Islamic world together, a world which today comprises more than a billion people.[12] Its grammar and its vocabulary explain the fact that Arabic is the only existing language whose 1400-year-old texts (including the Qur'an) can be read by commonly educated people, without depending on a translation into something like 'new high Arabic'.

The Qur'an has now become a sort of 'super weapon' (*Die Zeit,* Hamburg). After the Gulf War, it was the bestseller of 1991.[13] This is not necessarily a positive development, however, because Qur'anic studies without guidance can be counter-productive, and because there is a second source of Islamic knowledge: the traditions of the Prophet.

The Qur'an can only be properly understood if one is familiar with the historical context of individual revelations and with the coherent inner thread of the text. Commentaries frequently offer quite different viewpoints, according to whether they follow literal or 'hidden' meanings, Shi'ah or Sunni tendencies, or are written by a mystic or a rationalist,[14] by al Tabari of the ninth or Muhammad Asad of the twentieth century.[15]

Equally important is the knowledge of what the Prophet of Islam, a man of the highest integrity, authority, spirituality, and charisma[16] said, did, or consciously did not do (*Hadith*); for as the receiver of the message he was its born interpreter in cases of doubt. In addition, the Qur'an specifically demands that Muslims follow Muhammad's example in matters of faith and ethics. Islamic piety has turned this endeavor into the imitation of secondary details (like wearing a beard, methods of dental care, a preference for honey, etc.). This includes male circumcision, which, though not

---

12. For a national breakdown according to the *Yearbook of the Encyclopedia Britannica,* 1996, see pp. 310-311, which shows that Muslims in the world constitute one-fifth of the world's population (1,126,525,000).

13. Susanne Mayer, "Die Wunderwaffe," *Die Zeit,* 15 February 1991.

14. For a good overview of the subject see Muh. Surty, "A Survey of Tafsir Exegesis Literature in Arabic," *Muslim World Book Review,* Leicester 1987, no. 4, pp. 51ff; Rabah Stambouli, "Le commentaire coranique," in *El-Moujahid,* Algiers 30.3. and 1–4 April 1990; Mahmoud M. Ayoub, *The Qur'an and Its Interpreters,* vol. I and II, Albany, NY, 1984, 1992; and Neal Robinson, *Discovering the Qur'an,* London, 1996.

15. Al-Tabari, *The Commentary of the Qur'an,* vol. 1, Oxford 1987; Muh. Asad, *op. cit.,* footnote 2.

16. On the personality of Muhammad, see Ibn Ishāq/Ibn Hishām, *The Life of Muhammad,* Oxford 1955; Muhammad Hussein Haikal, *Haiyat Muhammad,* Cairo, 1936 (with many translations); Martin Lings, *Muhammad,* New York, 1981; Virgil Gheorghiu, *La vie de Mahomet,* Paris 1970; Emile Dermenghem, *Mahomet,* Paris 1960; Karen Armstrong, *Muhammad. A Western Attempt to Understand Islam,* London 1991.

mentioned in the Qur'an, is honored as a practice rooted in the Old Testament.

In some circles this natural, pious veneration of Muhammad—the precious tool chosen by God for His last revelation—has led to exalted and speculative forms of glorification, in particular, during the celebration of his birthday (*al mawlid al nabawī*), which is not entirely harmless given the career of Jesus during the development of Christology. This modest Arab, who on the occasion of the first revelation ('Read!. . .') in the "Night of Power" (*Laylat al Qadr*) admitted that he was *unlettered* and who always emphasized his mere humanity, has been portrayed as incapable of sinning, even as pre-existential cosmic light (the light of Muhammad), surrounded by myth and legend.[17]

Only the study of the several ḥadith collections, based on their specific science of tradition, permits one to gain a full understanding of Islamic moral teachings in all of their complexity. Only the practice of this 'sunnah' makes the specific *homo islamicus* and Islamic civilization.[18] It is not possible to describe this world here in detail. For our purposes it is more important to examine the significant differences between the Islamic and the Western, Christian-based image and understanding of man and morals in our day.

Despite the fundamental ethical feelings we have in common—virtues such as fraternity, honesty, pity, generosity, discretion, etc.—it is possible to isolate six major differences between the two:

1. A Muslim lives in a world without clergy and without religious hierarchy; when he prays he does not pray via Jesus, Mary or other interceding saints, but directly to God—as a fully emancipated believer—and this in a religion free of mysteries. An atmosphere of this kind suits the modern democratic citizen come of age far better than the wondrous, mystery-stricken atmosphere of the Byzantine and Catholic Churches, geared towards 'intercession' and focusing on sacraments administered by clergymen.

---

17. Annemarie Schimmel, *Und Muhammad ist Sein Prophet,* Cologne 1981.

18. The most important Hadith collections are those of *al Bukhārī and Muslim*; complete translations are only available in English and French; see *Sahīh al Bukhārī,* 9 vols, Chicago 1976; *Sahīh Muslim,* 4 vols, Lahore 1976. Now also available on CD-ROM and PC-disks like "Sakhr" and "MacHadith" for the Macintosh. For complete descriptions of the Islamic faith I refer to Henri Laoust, *La profession de foi d'Ibn Taymiyya—La Wasitiyya,* Paris 1986; Muh. Abdou, *Risālat at Tawhīd,* Paris 1925; Muh. Hamidullah, *Initiation à l'Islam,* Algiers 1981.

2. With its absolute prohibition of pork, alcohol and other drugs Islam serves public health; it continues to insist on the fundamental responsibility of those who misuse addictive substances, instead of exculpating them as socially sick. The stress-reducing effect of regular contemplative prayer which structures a Muslim's day also contributes to the good physical and mental health of the individual and the whole society in a way unknown to Christian Sunday worship or morning prayer.

3. In contrast to St. Paul's condemnation of all matters sexual, defamation of marriage and the propagation of monasticism, which have been responsible for so much suffering, repression and guilt in the Christian world, Islam approves of clean and legitimate sexual activity without reservation. On the other hand, it does not approve of the over-reaction to the devastation wreaked by Paul—the modern 'sex wave' characterized by complete lack of inhibition. This composure corresponds to the fact that, in contrast to the West, Islam continues to abide by and defend the natural gender roles of men and women, in the conviction that it is not possible to act against the basics of nature for very long without risking catastrophe (see the chapters "Woman in Society" and "The Veiled Orient").

4. With its commandment to love thy neighbor as thyself, Christianity makes a demand impossible to fulfill by the average person, but which weighs heavily on his conscience; this, like the demonization of sexuality, leads to an intensification of the negative psychological consequences of the fateful Christian doctrine of original sin, up to a point where it becomes possible to manipulate the masses thanks to their sense of culpability. In contrast to this, Islam is a religion of the golden mean, whose commandments (Ramadan, daily prayer, etc) are not easy, but possible for everyone to fulfill. In addition, Islam does not teach Muslims to regard themselves as requiring salvation. Mass sociology has taught us the potentially evil consequences of a redemption syndrome.

5. The attitude of Muslims to business and work is socially oriented, not primarily focused on efficiency; it may therefore be regarded as a corrective to the derailing of industrial society. This is particularly true of the Qur'anic insistence on sharing profit and loss (see the chapter "The Islamic Market Economy").

6. Finally, the general attitude of Muslims, even toward a pluralistic, secular State should be one of exemplary tolerance, despite the latter's materialistic outlook and claim to be the only road to universal happiness (see the chapter "Tolerance or Violence?")—in keeping with the last vers-

es of *Sūrat al Kāfirūn* (109). This should indeed be pinned above the desk of every Muslim, Christian, atheist and agnostic, and also of the author of this book, before entering into any comparison of whatever system of belief:

> **I will not worship that which you have worshipped, Nor will you worship that which I worship. To you be your way and to me mine!**[19]

---

19. Translation issued by the King Fahd Complex for the Printing of the Holy Qur'an, Al Madinah, 1992.

THE ISLAMIC VIEW OF
CHRISTIANITY

Whenever a Muslim pronounces or reads the name of the Prophet Muhammad, also while reading this book, he always wishes peace and blessing upon him.[1] He should do the same whenever he utters the name of Jesus.

This might come as some surprise to readers unfamiliar with Islam's view of itself. Islam is not to be understood as a newer, younger religion than Christianity, but as the completion and reaffirmation of Abraham's pristine monotheism (42:13). Islam may thus be regarded as both the youngest *and* the oldest of the three world religions. In fact, quite apart from its basic tolerance,[2] Islam does not claim exclusiveness for itself as the Catholic Church still does in practice even after the second Vatican Council. Rather, recognizing all earlier prophets as a matter of principle and conviction,[3] Islam builds on the valid core of all earlier revelations;[4] in the words of Paul Schwarzenau, "the Qur'an is an ecumenical revelation".[5] God states in the Qur'an:

> **Say: We believe in Allah and in what has been sent down to us, and what was sent down to Abraham, Ishmael, Isaac, and Jacob and the sons of Jacob, and what was given to Moses, Jesus and the Prophets from their Lord. We make no distinction between any of them and to Him have we submitted. (3:84)[6]**

The validity of Islam is not built on a rejection of the other two Semitic religions but derives from their comparison.[7] In fact Islam, Judaism and

---

1. *Ṣalla Allāhu 'alayhi wa sallam.* (God, bless Muhammad and grant him peace.)
2. See the chapter 'Tolerance or Violence?'
3. Qur'an 2:87; 6:83–87.
4. Qur'an 33:7; 5:46.
5. Paul Schwarzenau, *Korankunde für Christen,* second edition, Hamburg 1990. The author is Professor Emeritus of Protestant Theology.
6. Translation by Muhammad Taqi-ud-Din Al-Hilali and Muhammad Muhsin Khan, *Interpretation of the Meanings of the Noble Qur'an in the English Language,* Riyadh, 1993.
7. See Emanuel Kellerhans, *Der Islam,* second edition, Basel 1956, pp. 377 f.

Christianity are related religions, whose differences are small in comparison to Buddhism and Hinduism.[8]

This explains why Muslims feel entitled to consider Jesus as a prophet
of Islam, though not the last one. Because he "submitted totally to God's
will," quintessentially he was indeed a 'Muslim'.[9] Islamic theology
teaches that Muhammad (*Ahmad*) was announced not only in the Old
Testament, but by Jesus, too, as the last prophet to seal all revelation
(33:40).[10]

Islam's view of Jesus and Mary stems primarily from the third and the
nineteenth *surahs* of the Qur'an,[11] but (and this is less well-known) also
from the Islamic tradition (*Sunnah*). Both focus on Jesus' and Mary's
unique function in the history of divine intervention and are, therefore,
less narrative than archetypal:

> **And mention Mary in the book. When she drew aside . . . We sent
> to her Our angel of revelation and he appeared to her as a perfect
> human being . . . She said: "How can I have a son when no man has
> ever touched me?" (19:16–20).**

> **He said: "Thus it is: God creates what He wills. When He wills a
> thing to be, He merely says to it: 'Be!' and it is. And He will teach
> him the scripture, and wisdom, and the Torah, and the Gospel."
> (3:47f.)**

> **(He will say:) . . . I shall heal the blind and the leper and bring the
> dead back to life with God's permission. (3:49)**

---

8. This is how Father Gregor Böckermann sees it as well. See *Frankfurter Allgemeine
Zeitung*, 25 September 1986, p. 11.

9. See William E. Phipps, *Muhammad and Jesus: A Comparison of the Prophets and
Their Teachings*, London, 1996; Muh. Ata ur-Rahim, *Jesus, A Prophet of Islam*, third edition, London 1983; Ahmad Abdel-Wahab, *Dialogue Transtextuel entre le Christianisme
et l'Islam*, Paris 1987; Kenneth G. Robertson, *Jesus or Isa: A Comparison of the Jesus of
the Bible and the Jesus of the Koran*, New York 1983; Nilo Geagea, *Mary of the Koran:
A Meeting Point between Christianity and Islam*, New York 1984. A. von Denffer, *Der
Islam und Jesus*, Munich 1991.

10. This is based on John 14,26 and John 16,13 with the assumption that Parakletos
(supporter, comforter) should actually read Periklytos—in Arabic 'Ahmad'. See David
Benjamin, *Muhammad in der Bibel*, Munich 1987, pp. 183ff.; Sahib Mustaqim Bleher,
Das Zeugnis der Bibel–Biblische Stellen weisen auf die Wahrheit des Koran, Weilerswist,
1984, pp. 18, Schwarzenau, *op. cit.*

11. See also 2: 116f; 21: 26–30.

Clearly, Muslims see Jesus as a miracle-working, divinely inspired (5:110) prophet in the Jewish tradition; not begotten (112:3; 72:3) but created by divine intervention; born of Mary, the Virgin. He is *not* regarded as a pre-existential, consubstantial, divine 'Son of God' as taught by the doctrine of incarnation, but as His chosen servant (*'abd*):

> They say: "God has taken (unto Him) a son." Glorified be He! He has no needs. (10:68) [12]

> And they say: "The Most Gracious has taken a son (for Himself)." Certainly, you have made a monstrous allegation. (19:88)

The Qur'an clearly rejects any idea of a divine Trinity (5:72–75), including a *de facto* divinization of Mary (5:116–118) which might result from an excessive adoration of her (of which the dogma of her ascension to Heaven is an example).[13] Like her son, Mary was "a sign for the world" (21:91) and "one of the obedient ones" (66:12), no more and no less:

> ... and do not say "three". Refrain (from that) ... God is but one God. (4:171)

The Qur'an confirms Jesus' ascension to heaven (4:158) which, however, was not preceeded by his death on the cross as described in the Gospels (4:157).

How may the rejection of the divine nature of Jesus, of the personalized 'Holy Spirit' and of the Trinity be regarded today? I believe that Islam will win supporters from the Christian camp, especially in this regard.

In everyday Christian life the 'Holy Spirit' hardly plays a role any more. It is becoming evident that this divine 'person' is an intellectual construct, owing its postulation to Platonic and Gnostic notions, but also to Neoplatonic ideas which had belatedly infiltrated the Church. I refer less to Isis/Osiris/Horus than to Plato's God/Demiurge/Logos and to the trilogy existence/reason/soul of Plotinus and Proclus. The author of the Gospel of

---

12. Translation by Marmaduke Pickthall, *The Meaning of the Glorious Qur'an: Explanatory Translation,* Revised and Edited in Modern Standard English by Dr. Arafat El Ashi, amana publications, Beltsville, MD, 1996.

13. In the religion as practiced, Mary has certainly relegated the Holy Spirit to fourth place. That it is possible for Muslim Sufi to give in to excessive adoration of Mary is clear from the cosmic hymn to her by Charles-André Gilis, *Marie en Islam,* Paris 1990.

John, whoever he was, obviously breathed thin speculative air: "In the beginning was the Word and the Word was with God and God was the Word. . ."

The philosophical figure of the 'Logos' as a third divine person made its entry into the text of the New Testament through a process of creative translation. The relevant word 'comforter' was first rendered as 'spirit' and then, in capital letters, as 'Holy Spirit'.[14]

'Logos' or 'spirit' is, however, described throughout the New Testament as something other than a person, amongst other things as 'the spirit of God' (1. Cor. 2: 10–12) and as a 'gift' (Luke 11:13). At any rate, Jesus never referred to a Trinity which after all would have been for him a fundamental matter; he, like all Jewish Christians, apparently harbored the Jewish idea of a unitary God.[15]

As is well known, all this did not prevent the first ecumenical Council of Nicaea (325) from establishing a Trinity, an act which was not declaratory but constitutive—nevertheless a man-made dogma and no more. But it eliminated all early Christian literature which contradicted this construction.

Just as important (or tragic) is the fact that the oldest surviving manuscripts of the New Testament were all written *after* the Council. Although one does not necessarily have to agree with Karlheinz Deschner, who refers to the 'criminal history of Christianity,' his thesis of a 'falsified religion' corresponds closely to Muslim theory.[16]

As far as the ontological status of *Jesus* and his role as a savior are concerned, the situation is similar. Today, not only Protestant theologians, but also some Catholic ones, no longer delude themselves about the precarious nature of the sources from which the historicity of Jesus might be established, let alone the countless contradictions and anachronisms in the Gospels and the subsequent introduction of heathen notions into Christian practice. The evidence is so poor that scientific research has even put into doubt whether Jesus was ever put on trial. At any rate, there

---

14. John 14,16 and 14,25 lend themselves for this operation; cf. Bleher, *op. cit.*, pp. 18–22, Benjamin *op. cit.*, pp. 180ff.

15. See Adolf Schlatter, *Die Geschichte der ersten Christenheit*, Gütersloh 1892; John Hick and Edmund S. Meltzer (eds) *Three Faiths—One God: A Jewish, Christian, Muslim Encounter*, London 1986; Gerd Lüdemann, Ketzer. *Die andere Seite des frühen Chirstentums*, Stuttgart, 1995.

16. Karlheinz Deschner, *Der gefälschte Glaube*, Munich 1988; Deschner, *Kriminalgeschichte des Christentums*, Hamburg, vol. 1, 1986; vol. 2, 1988.

are few reliable facts about his death, since there were no eye-witnesses at his burial and ascension.[17]

This situation helps to explain the 'Jesus boom' in contemporary literature, the index of which runs to some 500 pages for the past thirty years alone.

Even more precarious is the evidence regarding incarnation. In a correct translation of the New Testament the unbiased reader would not find a single reference allowing him to infer a divine nature of Jesus. He and God are not treated as identical. Indeed, the opposite is the case, not only at Golgotha, but in general. Even in John, Jesus says: "I ascend unto my Father and your Father; and to my God and your God" (20: 17).

We should not read much into terms such as 'father' and 'son,' for they are used allegorically in all religions for allegorizing the relationship with God, our creator.

Against this background it is possible today to distinguish at least four Christologies within the Churches:

1. A majority of simple believers, especially in rural areas, practice monotheism, in which God is more or less identical with Jesus. This anthropomorphic idea of God—the Unfathomable as infant in the crib—stems from our desire to worship something which is not so very different from ourselves. (It was *this* God whom Nietzsche could have killed!)

2. In the Protestant world in particular, even amongst the clergy, Jesus is regarded less and less as God, and more and more as a pure but exalted human being who set standards by living according to the principle of brotherly love, a touching man whom it is worth emulating, whether or not he so existed: after all, has Christian-Humanistic philosophy not proven itself as a value in and by itself?

    Thus, Jesus is in danger of being reduced to become the prototype of the ideal social worker, suffering like us, and with us, within the framework of a theology of misery.

3. At the opposite pole to this is a Christology which conjures up a 'cosmic' or 'mythological' Jesus, thus seeking (and finding) refuge in mystery and mysticism from insoluble hermeneutical problems.

    This, at any rate, is how I read authors like the American ex-Dominican Matthew Fox and Rüdiger Altmann, when the latter

---

17. See Weddig Fricke, "Standrechtlich gekreuzigt," *Person und Prozess des Jesus von Galiläa,* Frankfurt 1986; Gerd Lüdemann, *Die Auferstehung Jesu,* Göttingen, 1994.

writes of a 'Mystery of the night' "in which a God (sic) was born" and who professes a 'Gnosis of Christianity'.[18] Believers of this kind are satisfied with the sources as they are, as long as they can serve as something on which to hang the mythologies of God, the Great Mother, Light, Sin, and Salvation. Theologists of this kind have no inhibitions about speaking of "God realizing Himself fully through becoming man," and of maintaining, without fear of blasphemy, that "He, God, became someone else through incarnation."[19]

4. Finally, there is the tendency represented by John Hick and the Swiss theologian Hans Küng. They and many others admit the fragility of the original texts of Christianity courageously and with no illusions, but do not seek refuge in gnostic illumination or banal worldliness. Rather, they attempt to solve historical and ontological problems by a process of sacrificing untenable dogmas via new definitions. This leads to Jesus being reinterpreted as 'chosen and authorized by God,' and the Trinity becoming 'God's revelation in Jesus Christ through the Spirit'.[20]

Küng thus drew the obvious conclusion from his recognition of "how great the distance is between the original statements about Father, Son, and Spirit and the later dogmatic Church teachings on Trinity" and "how different the Christological conceptions are already within the New Testament". He admits quite frankly that there is scarcely anything in it which might suggest even remotely, a doctrine of Trinity.[21]

If the genuine intention of this Christology is to say that Jesus is neither begotten by God nor consubstantial with him, and that God's spirit does not represent a divine person, then it is Islamic and confirms the frequently heard assertion that "Muslims are the better Christians," in line with the earliest (Jewish) Christians. As rediscovered by Küng, only in the Qur'an has the Christology of the Jewish Christians been preserved pure and unadulterated.

---

18. Rüdiger Altmann, *Frankfurter Allgemeine Zeitung,* supplement of 21 December 1985.

19. Hans Waldenfels, *Frankfurter Allgemeine Zeitung,* 24. November 1985.

20. Hans Küng and J. van Ess, "Christianity and World Religions: paths of dialogue with Islam, Hinduism and Buddhism," Vol 1 *Islam,* translated by Peter Heinegg, London 1987; John Hick, *An Interpretation of Religion* (many editions).

21. Hans Küng, *Zu einem künftigen Dialog zwischen Christen und Muslimen, Universitas,* Stuttgart, 1984, p. 1351.

This new/old understanding of the nature and role of Jesus as a prophet is awe-inspiring, because to encounter a prophet among fellow human beings is indeed awe-inspiring. Yet this understanding of Jesus requires of its representatives to explain why they nevertheless continue to see themselves as, and to profess themselves to be, 'Christians'.[22]

In my opinion this loyalty has something to do with the Christian dogma of salvation and deliverance, based on the doctrine of original sin, and Jesus' Passion.

Islam rejects the idea of original sin because it is fatalistic, because it assumes that God's creation failed, and because it contradicts the Qur'anic principle that no one is made to carry someone else's burden; this certainly excludes the idea that mankind in its entirety, throughout the ages, was to be collectively responsible for acts committed by Adam and Eve. Ideas of this kind are in violation of the Islamic image of God.[23]

Islam denies the necessity of salvation and regards as blasphemous a theology of sacrificial death which states "In the death on the cross in which all humans' suffering is accumulated, God takes their sufferings upon Himself in order to save them".[24] For a theology of this kind assumes that God was unable to 'save' humankind without the creation of a second divine person for the purpose of his suffering. This idea—God as victim of mankind rebelling against Him—is in violation of the Islamic image of God as well.

Given these circumstances I agree with Paul Schwarzenau, when he characterizes the Muslims' denial of Jesus's death on the cross as a protest against the Christian ideology of the cross in general.[25] In the Muslim view of things it was not the Jews who killed Jesus, even if that is how it appeared to them, and Jesus did not suffer death on the cross, but was called by God at a later point in time and raised up to Heaven:

---

22. Hans Küng, *Why am I still a Christian?*, Edinburgh 1987, explains this in pedagogical terms.

23. For the function of original sin in Church history see Elaine Pagels, *Adam, Eva und die Schlange. Die Theologie der Sünde*, Reinbek 1990; also Isma'il al Faruqi, *Christian Ethics: A Historical and Systematic Analysis of Its Dominant Ideas*, McGill University Press 1967.

24. See Karl-Alfred Odin, *Frankfurter Allgemeine Zeitung*, leader of 4. 4. 1985; France has even seen the rise of a theology of a powerless God who constantly suffers with the poor, thus Jean Delumeau, *Ce que je crois*, Paris 1985.

25. Schwarzenau, *loc. cit*, p. 110.

God said: "O Jesus! I shall cause you to die and shall exalt you unto Me . . ." (3:55)

What actually happened at the scene of crucifixion no one knows despite many apocryphal speculations:[26]

They have no knowledge, but follow mere conjecture; and they have certainly not killed him. Rather, God has exalted him unto Himself, and Allah is Almighty, Allwise. (4:157 f.)[27]

For this reason the legend of the life and death of Jesus as an old man in Kashmir should be accepted for what it is.[28]

This, then, is the background to the highly topical question of what chance a Christian–Islamic dialogue, imperative for the maintenance of world peace, might have.[29]

"No world peace without religious peace." Hans Küng called a lecture on this subject held in Algiers on 22 November 1988, although he could not have known what would happen two years later in the Persian (or Arabian) Gulf. His hope is for a 'world ethos of nations' based on religious rapprochement and understanding—not a single religion, not a syncretic mixture, but global ethics.

A lot of preparatory work for this dialogue has been done, particularly on the part of Christians, on issues of substance[30] as well as on the atmosphere conducive to dialogue. This includes the interconfessional meetings in Cordoba, respectful publications by members of religious

---

26. See Hamza Boubakeur's intelligent commentary on 4:157 in his French translation of the Qur'an, third edition, Paris 1985; also G. Parrinder, *Jesus in the Qur'an,* Oxford 1977. He places the emphasis not on the 'not killed' but on the 'they have', i.e., he suggests that the exterior course of events could have corresponded to Christian portrayals and have been quite different in reality; Ahmed Deedat believes that Jesus was bound to the cross without dying on it: *Crucifixion or Cruci-Fiction?* Durban, S.A., 1985.

27. See Muh. Asad, *The Message of the Qur'an,* Gibraltar 1980, footnote 171 to 4:157; Yusuf Ali, *The Meaning of the Holy Qur'an,* 8th edition, Beltsville 1996, footnote 663 to 4:157. Both conclude that Jesus—whatever happened—did not die on the cross.

28. Andreas Faber-Kaiser, *Jesus lebte und starb in Kashmir,* Lucerne, 1986.

29. On the subject of the Christian-Islamic dialogue, see S. M. Abdullah, *Islam: für das Gespräch mit Christen,* 3rd edition, Altenberge 1990.

30. See *Im Gespräch: Islam und Christentum,* Cologne 1983; Maurice Borrmans, *Wege zum christlich-islamischen Dialog,* Frankfurt 1985; H.M. Baagil, *Christian Muslim Dialogue,* Birmingham, 1984; *Trialogue of the Abrahamic Faiths,* amana publications, ed. Isma'il R. al Faruqi, Beltsville, MD, 1995.

orders such as Michel Lelong,[31] the Pope's annual greetings to Muslims on the occasion of the feast of fast-breaking (*'Īd al Fiṭr*), and his invitation to a prayer community in Assisi on 27 October 1986.

But mutual understanding presupposes that both sides accept each other as each side sees itself. For Muslims, this means that they should not accuse Christians of being polytheists, despite what, from an Islamic point of view, appears to be a qualified monotheism. Christians in turn are required to scrap the intolerable doctrine *extra ecclesiam nullum salus* (no salvation outside the Church), not only formally, as occurred in Vatican II, but mentally too. This is unlikely for as long as the Catholic Church adheres to the principle of *extra ecclesiam nullus propheta* (no prophets outside the Church), accepting Islam as a path to 'Salvation' without accepting Muhammad so far as a guide on that path. In fact, one of Vatican II's inconsistencies was that it decided to regard even Muslims 'with respect,' yet carefully avoided any reference to the Qur'an and the man who transmitted it.[32]

From this state of affairs we can already see that rapprochement on theological matters is likely to remain limited, as long as there remain hard core, inflexible and therefore non-negotiable conflicting positions.

As Hans Küng observed in his Cordoba lecture, these are:
• the divine nature of Jesus for Christians;
• the divine revelation of the Qur'an for Muslims;
• the divine link between God and His 'Chosen People' for Jews;

Indeed, the contrast is clear: at the center of Christianity is a person, at the center of Islam is a book and at the center of Judaism is a pledge. From this point of view, God's Word was made flesh in Christianity, in Islam God's Word became a book.[33]

In as much as this is true, a theological reconciliation is only conceivable if Christianity adopts Küng's understanding of Jesus and accepts the Qur'an as a Holy Book.

This does not mean that there is no point in ecumenical dialogue, as long as non-negotiable aspects are excluded. One should never underestimate the value of small steps and the practical value of meetings on a human level, especially with guest workers or immigrants, as long as no

---

31. Michel Lelong, *Si Dieu l'avait voulu . . .* Paris 1986.
32. Hans Küng, *Christentum und Islam, Zeitschrift für Kulturaustausch,* Stuttgart, 1985, no. 3, pp. 311 ff.
33. Hans Küng, *Die Welt,* Hamburg, 6 March 1989, p. 13.

one harbors the ulterior motive of proselyting. It is a well-known fact, attested to by White Fathers and Sisters in North Africa, that Muslims can hardly be converted to Christianity, at any rate.

It is an entirely different question whether the Islamo-Christian dialogue, in case of success, would be relevant. This is a fully justified question because de-Christianization, especially in Europe, has progressed to such a point that both Muslims *and* Christians now seem to be minorities, sharing the same boat in an ocean of materialism, agnosticism, and atheism. This is a world which lacks any antenna for dialoguing with people of religion.

BELIEF AND KNOWLEDGE

The dream of 'my home is my castle' has materialized in Islam. Eavesdropping, spying on or annoying your neighbors is not allowed. If you have knocked three times and they have still not answered the door, leave them in peace. In short: mind your own business.[1]

But the thirst for knowledge, intellectual curiosity, is something quite different: according to both Qur'an and Sunnah the quest for knowledge is an attitude typical of every Muslim.

On dozens of occasions the Qur'an encourages us to use our reason and faculty of understanding in order to increase our knowledge (20:14):

Will you not use your reason? (2:44)

Do you not see . . . ? (31:20)

Do you not then reflect? (6:50)

It is possible to read the very first revelation to Muhammad—verses 1–5 of *Sūrat al 'Alaq* (96)—as an appeal to acquire reading and writing skills, to become literate:

Read, for your Lord is the most Generous One, Who taught (to write) with the pen, Taught man what he did not know (96:3–5).

The true, pensive Muslim thinks about God and creation "standing, sitting and lying down," he strives for objectivity, regardless of personal preferences, demanding evidence, not mere conjecture.[2] Similarly, according to a very popular Muslim maxim one ought to acquire knowledge even if that meant travelling to China.[3] Nowadays to follow suit might correspond to a journey to the moon. The Prophet greatly respected knowledge and learning; he is reported to have said:

---

1. See Qur'an 24:27 and the Prophet's Hadiths in *Ṣaḥīḥ Muslim* No. 5354 ff, and Hadith no. 12 in *Al Nawāwi, Forty Hadith*, Leicester, 3rd edition, 1977.

2. 3:191, 28:75, 30:29, 43:20, 45:24.

3. This saying is not based on an authentic hadith but popular nevertheless.

On the Day of Judgement the ink of the scholars and the blood of the religious martyrs will be weighed—and the ink of the scholars will weigh more
than the blood of the martyrs.[4]

The Prophet's companions, including the first Caliphs, took this call
seriously, as was beautifully illustrated by 'Ali ibn Abi Talib's response
to the question whether he used any written documents other than the
Qur'an. "No," he replied, "nothing other than Allah's book, the power of
understanding given to every Muslim and one piece of paper" (with notes
about three decisions of the Prophet).[5]

This joyful curiosity, combined with a readiness always to exert one's
mind, was the right platform for the extraordinary development of the
Islamic sciences from the late eighth century onwards, a mere fourteen
striking examples of which are outlined below:[6]

• Ibn Firnas (died 888) to whom the first flying machine is attributed;

• Muhammad b. Musa al Khwarizmi (died 846), father of algebra (*al
jabr*) and of the algorithm—this term being a corruption of his name;

• Abu Bakr al Razi/Rhazes (864–935), whose medical work *Mansuri,*
the *Liber Almansoris,* was used for centuries in European universities;

• The philosopher and physician Ibn Sina/Avicenna (980–1037), whose
medical encyclopedia was still in use in European universities in the early
nineteenth century;

• Al Hasan b. al Haytham/Alhazen (965–1039), inventor of the camera
obscura;

• Abu al Rayhan al Biruni (973–1050), universal genius on a par with
Goethe, historian of science, diplomat, student of Sanskrit, astrologer,
mineralogist, pharmacologist, etc.;

• Umar al Khayyam (died between 1123 and 1131), poet and mathe-
matician. He also reformed the Indian calendar with greater accuracy than
the 1582 Gregorian calendar;

---

4. *Kanz al 'Ummal,* vol. 10, hadiths 28899–28902; Abdülkadir Karahan, *Kirk Hadis,*
Istanbul 1991, Hadith 22, p. 52. See also *Ihyā 'Ulūm al Dīn, Book of Worship,* English
trans. by Fazlul Karim.

5. *Ṣaḥīḥ al Bukhārī,* "Book of Knowledge (III)," Hadith 111.

6. See for details Joseph Schacht and C. E. Bosworth, *Das Vermächtnis des Islams,* 2
vols, Munich 1983; Thomas Arnold and Arthur Guillaume, *The Legacy of Islam,* Oxford
1931; Marshall G. S. Hodgson, *The Venture of Islam,* vol. 2, Chicago 1974; Alistair
Crombie, "Griechisch-arabische Naturwissenschaften und abendländisches Denken," in
Europa und der Orient 800–1900, Gütersloh 1989.

• The jurist/philosopher Ibn Rushd/Averroës (1126–1198) who, as a multiple commentator on Aristotle, had a great influence on Western philosophy (and who also discovered sunspots in his spare time);[7]

• The Egyptian physician Ibn al Nafis (died 1288) who discovered blood circulation;

• Ibn Baṭṭuṭah (1304–1368 or 1377), Moroccan globetrotter on a par with Marco Polo, who reached Timbuktu, Peking, and the Volga.

• The Andalusian Ibn Khaldun (1332–1406) whose introduction (al Muqaddimah) to his history of the world (kitāb al 'Ibar) made him both the founder of sociology and of modern historiography, introducing a revolutionary critique of traditional historical sources;[8]

• The navigator Ahmad Ibn Majid, fifteenth-century authority on ocean voyages.

• The Turkish ocean geographer and admiral Piri Reis (1480–1553), whose Kitab-i Bahriye, with its precise maps of the seas, still amazes us,[9] and his scientific colleague Seyyidi Ali Reis (died 1562) who measured the Asiatic coasts and developed nautical astronomy.

This short list alone shows that it was not the Occident which inherited the Hellenistic civilization, but the Islamic world. In view of the explosion of knowledge and technology in the Islamic world, it is self-evident that cultural exchange in the Middle Ages was a one-way street. In fact, the Muslims could find hardly anything worth learning from the Occident (Marshall Hodgson). The West was a 'net importer'—from the windmill and troubadours' songs to the 'Gothic' pointed arch. This cultural imperialism and one-sided globalization—as we would call it today—quite naturally left traces in European languages. When we speak of admiral, algebra, cipher, amalgam, alcohol, lute, guitar, alcove, muslin or tariff we are still using Arabic vocabulary today.

But the Islamic arts and sciences, especially the natural sciences, faded during the fourteenth century. One reason for this was the emerging theory of taqlīd, the voluntary "closing of the doors of (free) interpretation," discussed in the chapter "Fundamentalism": a theory which led to the de facto atrophy of research in favor of the preservation (and recapitulation) of what was already known. According to this theory, everything that

7. Ibn Rushd's competence in jurisprudence, especially comparative law, was equally impressive; see Ibn Rushd—The Distinguished Jurist's Primer, trans. Imran A. Khan Nyazee, 2 vol., Reading, 1994, 1996.
8. The Muqqadimah, translated by Franz Rosenthal, Princeton 1976.
9. Kitab-i Bahriye Piri Reis, Istanbul 1988.

should be known and was worth knowing was already known and better understood by those closer in time to the revelation.

Parts of the Qur'an and Sunnah could be interpreted in this way. Thus, the verse: **"We have no knowledge but that which You have taught us"** (2:32) could be understood to mean that any attempt to find knowledge not contained in the Qur'an is inappropriate. Does God not speak of a type of learning which **"does not benefit them"** (2:102), useless knowledge, so to speak?

This explains the hostility towards science and philosophy expressed by some Islamic scholars (*'ulamā*) who made much of the fact that the Prophet consciously and repeatedly refused to answer questions. From the fifteenth century onwards this attitude inevitably led to a certain doctrine of abstinence from knowledge in a number of respects.[10]

This trend was intensified by the fear of introducing bad things through forbidden innovation (*bid'ah*). According to the Sunnah a distinction should be made on principle between desirable, good innovation (*bid'ah ḥasanah*) and prohibited, bad innovation (*bid'ah sayyi'ah*). In the Afterlife serious punishments are reserved for those who introduced the latter. Soon, however, every innovation was suspected of being inadmissible; and the term *bid'ah* took on the general meaning of 'bad innovation':[11]

> Beware of new things; for every new thing is an innovation and every innovation a mistake . . .[12]

As the Middle Ages progressed, the allegation of *bid'ah* became a formidable weapon against progress.

The extent to which this is still a burning issue, curbing the ability of Islamic States to react to modern challenges, is shown by the fact that Prof. Hassan Ben Saddik (Tangiers) was asked to hold a lecture on the issue before King Hassan II in Rabat on 24 March 1991. The aim was apparently to remind the public that the traditions in question referred to

10. Al Nawawi, *op. cit.*, ḥadith no. 30.

11. Lately, when after prayer in Riyadh I wanted to shake hands with my neighbors in the mosque, saying *"taqabbala Allahu!"* (May God accept [your prayer]), I, too, was accused by them of *'bid'ah'*.

12. Al Nawawi, *op. cit.*, ḥadith no. 28; see also no. 5 and *Saḥīḥ Muslim. Aḥadith* nos. 6466–6470.

theological and ethical innovations only, and did not stand in the way of *technological* progress.[13]

Of course, the decline which took place from the fourteenth century onwards was not entirely without rays of hope. There were creative spirits at work even during this period particularly in the theological, literary and architectural worlds. (We need only to think of the Taj Mahal (1634) and the Blue Mosque in Istanbul, built at the same time). To mention but a few, they were thinkers like the Indian Shaykh Wali Allah (1703–1763), Muhammad b. 'Abd al Wahhab (1703–1787) in Arabia and Amadu Bamba (1850–1927) in Senegal, all forerunners of fundamentalist and purist reform movements. The brotherhoods that now dominate West Africa, the Murīdīyya and Tijanīyah or Ahmadīyah, for whom Fes has become the center, were also founded during the period of decline.

But these rays of hope were darkened by the significant lack of Islamic natural scientists and the reactionary activities of *'ulama'* hostile to any kind of innovation. In 1580 in Istanbul, they had the observatorium destroyed, erected only the year before. As late as 1745, they succeeded in prohibiting the first printing press in the Islamic world, which had existed in the same city since 1728. It is hardly surprising that there were only 5,000 secondary school pupils in Egypt in 1875, but 11,000 students at the Al Azhar University, which offered a traditional education but was incompetent in the field of science.

As a consequence only one scientist hailing from the Islamic world has ever been awarded the Nobel prize—the Pakistani physicist Abdes-salam Ahmed.

Islamic philosophy has also frequently been accused of playing a major part in the decline of the intellectual life of the Ummah. Its fascinating history, however, does not warrant such unambiguous conclusions.[14]

---

13. The lecture, which I was allowed to attend, was published in four installments over the following days by *Le Matin du Sahara et du Maghrib* (Casablanca). The speaker established that, for example, minutes of silence (instead of 'prayers for the absent') and charity tombolas (because of gambling) are forbidden innovations.

14. See M. M. Sharif (ed.), *A History of Muslim Philosophy*, 2 vols, Wiesbaden 1963; Majid Fakhry, *A History of Islamic Philosophy*, London 1983; T. J. de Boer, *The History of Philosophy in Islam*, London 1903; Henry Corbin, *History of Islamic Philosophy*, London 1993; Georges Anawati, "Philosophie, Theologie und Mystik," in *Das Vermächtnis des Islams, op. cit.*; Oliver Leaman, *An Introduction to Medieval Islamic Philosophy*, Cambridge 1985; Murad W. Hofmann, *Zur Rolle der islamischen Philosophie*, Cologne 1984; Majid Fakhry, *Philosophy, Dogma and the Impact of Greek Thought in Islam*, Brookfield, Vermont, 1994.

Since the ninth century, under the influence of Greek philosophy, Muslims had been trying to turn the Qur'anic revelation (which, of course, is not a philosophical dissertation) into a comprehensive, rational system of thought. The school of the so-called Mu'tazilites, established in Baṣrah and Baghdad, increasingly integrated itself into the pattern of Greek thinking, but was still more philosophical theology than theological philosophy. The rationalists of the Mu'tazilah still accepted the thesis that "at the beginning was the Qur'an"; they accepted the existence of God and the revelatory nature of the Qur'an without question, not yet asking *whether* God existed, but rather, *how* He was and functioned.

But in their attempts to reconcile the Qur'an with Reason the Mu'tazilites soon entered the realm of metaphysical speculation and slid into heretical positions, even while they did not question the validity of Qur'anic statements which conflicted with their reasoning, but interpreted them as allegorical. Nevertheless, on their favorite subjects this led to attitudes which were regarded as blasphemous, scandalous, even insane by the Orthodoxy. According to the Mu'tazilah:

- God has no attributes in the sense of the 99 most beautiful names (see the chapter "Fatalism"); despite *ayah* 41:47 He knows only universals, no particulars;
- The world was not created (and is therefore eternal);
- The Qur'an is created;
- Man possesses free will as a co-creator (see the chapter "Fatalism"); 'evil' is his creation alone; and
- Man will not be physically resurrected.

Clearly, at that point Mu'tazilite philosophers no longer took the Qur'an, but their own logic as decisive criterion, drafting a bloodless, cerebral picture of God.

This rationalistic philosophy based on Aristotelean ideas reached its climax in the twelveth century with Averroës.[15]

It must have been no less worrying for the Orthodoxy that under the influence of Neoplatonism other Muslim philosophers were proceeding almost simultaneously on the path of 'illumination,' attempting to bring

---

15. Averroës, *Tahafut al Tahafut* (The Incoherence of the Incoherence), London 1978; Averroës, *On the Harmony of Religion and Philosophy*, London 1961; Hans Wilderotter, *Aristoteles, Averroës und der Weg der arabischen Philosophie nach Europa, in Europa und der Orient* 800–1900, Gütersloh, 1989.

Islam into accord with Gnosticism, the theory of immanation and light mysticism, as was the case with the three great intellectuals Abu Nasr Muhammad al Farabi/Alpharabius (c. 873–c. 950), Muhy al Din Ibn 'Arabi (1165–1240)[16] and Abu 'Ali al Husain b. Sina/Avicenna (980–1037).[17]

The counter-reaction, in the form of the Ash'arite school followed quickly. They denied the premises upon which the entire Mu'tazilite edifice of ideas was based, namely, the assumption that human perception and logic could lead to knowledge about metaphysical reality. Their leader Abu al Hasan al Ash'arī (873–935) not only made philosophy the servant of theology once more, but took all metaphysics, including thinking in terms of causality, to absurdity. According to al Ash'arī and Abu Hamid al Ghazali/Algazel (1058–1111)[18] who completed his work, all being exists in the absence of any laws of causality binding on God, unfathomable for man, as God's will, habit or imagination.

The final assault against speculative philosophy, bringing about its 'downfall,' was led by al Ghazali against Ibn Sina with his book on the *Incoherence of Philosophers* (*Tahāfut al Falāsifah*), which one generation later inspired the refreshing polemics of Ibn Rushd's *The Incoherence of Incoherence* (*Tahāfut al Tahāfut*). Since then it has been a maxim of Sunni Islam that any precise knowledge of God and His actions can only be gained through revelation (which eludes analysis) and cannot be obtained through reasoning. The Muslim must accept the word of God as he finds it, without, in philosophical hubris, asking 'how' .

Since then, the intellectual Muslim has renounced metaphysics; and 'Islamic' philosophy has existed only under the cloak of mysticism (often Shi'ah in nature), as in the Brotherhood of Purity (*Ikhwān al Ṣafā*) of Baṣrah[19] (see the chapter "Mysticism").

---

16. Ibn 'Arabi, *La Profession de Foi*, Paris 1985. Michel Chodkiewicz, *Un Océan sans Rivage, Ibn Arabi, Le Livre et la Loi*, Paris, 1992.

17. See Gerhard Endress, "Der erste Lehrer," Der arabische Aristoteles und das Konzept der Philosophie, in *Festschrift für A. Falaturi*, Cologne 1991, pp. 151ff.; and *Avicenna on Theology*, London 1951.

18. His moving "Confessions" entitled *Al Munqidh min al Ḍalāl* (Deliverance from Error) are very enlightening. See *The Confessions of Al Ghazzālī*, translated by Claud Field, Lahore 1978. For the most important of his more than 400 works, see *Ihyā' 'Ulūm al Dīn*, 4 vols; Lahore (no date); for mystical tendencies see al Ghazali's *Mishkāt al Anwār*, (The Niche for Lights), translated by W. H. T. Gairdner, New Delhi 1923; Farid Jabre, *La Notion de la Ma'rifa chez Ghazali*, Beirut 1958.

19. See Ikhwān al Ṣafā, *The Case of the Animals Versus Man before the King of the Jinn: A Tenth-century Ecological Fable of the Pure Brethren of Baṣrah*, translated by Lenn Evan Goodman, Boston 1978.

Thus orthodox 'counter philosophy' was no more (and did not want to be more) than radical epistemological theory, leading, via a rational agnosticism qualified by the Qur'an, to an intellectual humility which today—1000 years later—seems uncommonly modern. It was not Ludwig Wittgenstein in the twentieth century, but al Ash'arī in the ninth century who heralded the 'end of philosophy'. It was not David Hume and modern scientific theory, but the Ash'arites who first recognized the undemonstrability of the law of causality. It was not Immanuel Kant (*Critique of Pure Reason,* 1781) and the modern theorists of linguistic philosophy (philosophy as a 'language game') who first developed a radical epistemology, but the Muslim philosophers of the ninth century.

If the critical Western thinkers mentioned above did not trigger a decline in Western culture, how can we blame Islamic philosophy for the cultural decline of the Islamic world?

Against this background, let us now examine Islam's present attitude toward the other sciences, in particular, modern natural science.

Point of departure must be the Muslim conviction that real discrepancies between the results of scientific research and the Qur'an are precluded. Therefore, they attribute such discrepancies to misinterpretation—either of the Qur'an or of the results of research data.

The real problem in this context is the modern concept of science. Muslims not only accuse science of posing illegitimately as a substitute for religion, but also of making a bad job of it. Seyyed Hossein Nasr put this brilliantly at a conference of the Max Planck Society for Physics and Astrophysics in 1983:

> Islam cannot accept the reductionism of modern science, which reduces metaphysics to psychology, psychology to biology, biology to chemistry and chemistry to physics, therefore reducing all elements of reality to the lowest level of manifestation, the physical.

This requires clarification:

On the one hand, from the Islamic point of view, Western science is carried out too autonomously, as 'art for art's sake,' and with too great a degree of gullibility. *Extra scientiam nullum salus* (No salvation outside of the sciences) could well be many a scientist's profession of faith as a 'believer without religion'. He defines God in terms of gaps in verifiable knowledge, man as a risk factor in a technical environment, and the social system as a trivial machine. Thus, as the German philosopher Jürgen Habermas said, the moral code in the modern era, just like art, becomes an "embodiment of the principle of subjectivity".[20] Indeed, religion is frequently regarded in our 'scientific age' as a backward, irrational way of solving problems of the human psyche. Nietzsche wanted to kill God—that was bound to fail; scientists want to kill the belief in God—this may well succeed.

And yet empirical, positivist science cannot replace the religion it supplants when it comes to supplying meaning and to setting moral norms. In this sense, the two operate on totally different planes. Even with Sir Karl Popper's method of 'trial and error,' the continuous falsification of emerging hypotheses, science does not acquire normative competence, but remains bound to what is quantifiable. Morals are not physical functions, 'meaning' is not the result of a biochemical compound and love is terribly unscientific.

Indeed, in the ideological domain, science has led modern man only to skepticism, the loss of certainty, data fetishism and a latent identity crisis. At best, it can offer a sort of secularized post-Christian eschatology with its ideology of progress.[21] It produces questions *ad infinitum* without giving definitive answers, which once led André Malraux to ask whether "a civilization of questions and of the moment" could be viable? Michael Harrington's question is basically the same: "Where is there in our relativistic technological society a social ethic which can save us from our brilliance?"[22]

Muslims are not the only ones who object to this false development of science as a (bad) substitute for religion.[23] On the contrary, contemporary 'searchers for standards,' such as Hans-Georg Gadamer, Helmut Kuhn, and Daniel Bell are on this path. People speak of the return to metaphysics as a result of the belated recognition that the more enlightened the modern world becomes, the more indispensable religion is: at least in order to legitimize power and law, for ethical motivation and social coherence. In short: people are once again starting to recognize that the-

---

20. Jürgen Habermas, *Der philosophische Diskurs der Moderne*, Frankfurt 1985.

21. See Karl Loewith, *Meaning in History*, Chicago 1949.

22. Jürgen Habermas, *op. cit.*; Michael Harrington, *The Politics at God's Funeral: The Spiritual Crisis of Western Civilisation*, New York 1983.

23. See also amongst others Alfred North Whitehead, *Wie entsteht Religion?*, Frankfurt 1985; Jean-Francois Lyotard, *The Postmodern Condition*, Manchester 1986; Ernest Gellner, *Relativism and the Social Sciences*, Cambridge 1985.

ology and political sciences are mutually supportive and that the prediction of a demise of religion, to say the least, had been provincial.[24]

The collapse of Darwinism, Freudianism, Marxism and old physics contributed to this trend, especially since the brain will not succeed in researching the brain.[25] Scientists are becoming more modest since they have begun to recognize that so-called 'natural laws' may only represent approximations that the world is not a machine functioning according to our previous naive conception of causality, and that our brain dwarfs any gadget invented by Bill Gates.

In the opinion of many Muslim academics, even a science freed from its hubris is not value-neutral, and still has to be 'Islamized'. Their motto is to "introduce Islam into knowledge," and this has its own history.

The colonization of the Arab world led to the general adoption of Western civilization by the élites in the hope of catching up with the West; however, the result of assimilation was disappointing. Muslim students usually remained behind their Western counterparts in learning and, at the same time, lost the basis of their own civilization. Torn between two cultures, they became frustrated consumers of a foreign technology that they could not master.

The reactive negative result is a frequently encountered Third World technophobia. Western technology is demonized because it was developed in an atheistic environment and encourages a fundamentally skeptical and critical approach. In contrast, more level-headed Muslims point to the basic value-neutrality of technology and call for its selective use within the framework of an Islamic society.[26]

The call for the Islamization of knowledge pioneered by the International Institute for Islamic Thought (IIIT) in Herndon, VA, and by the International Islamic University of Kuala Lumpur, Malaysia, is more positive. It does not call for rejection of the Western model 'lock, stock and barrel,' but for Islamic education and university reform.[27]

---

24. Parvez Manzoor, "The Crisis of Intellect and Reason in the West," *The Muslim World Book Review*, Leicester, 1987, no. 2, p. 3; Daniel Bell, *The Cultural Contradictions of Capitalism*, London, 1976.

25. See. Ed. Quentin Skinner, *The Return of Grand Theory in the Human Sciences;* the main problem with brain research is the fact that perceptions take place there and not in the eyes or ears. Also see Karl R. Popper and John C. Eccles, *The Self and Its Brain—An Argument for Interactionism*, N.Y., NY, 1977.

26. This is the position, for example, of the Nobel Prize winner A. Abdessalam, 'Islam et Sciences', *El-Moujahid*, Algiers, 16 and 17. 4. 1989.

27. See *Islamization of Knowledge, General Principles and Workplan*, International Institute of Islamic Thought, 3rd edition, Herndon, VA, 1995; Dawud Assad, "The Islamization of Knowledge," in *The Muslim World*, 21. 12. 1985.

In fact, there is room for great improvement in the schools and universities of all Muslim countries, because the curriculum still relies too heavily on uncritical imitation. The authority of the teacher is still absolute, many questions remain taboo subjects, and rote learning is still encouraged. Islamic society as a whole—starting with each family's father—must understand that the prerequisite for scientific progress is a climate of creative freedom of thinking which should be encouraged even at kindergarten level. There is no other path—and there is certainly no short cut—to scientific achievement.

Unfortunately, some of the suggestions for the 'Islamization' of the sciences aim in the opposite direction, and are reminiscent of the bigoted attempts of 1930s Germany to further the 'German spirit' by 'cleansing mathematics from Jewish elements' and 'setting biology on an Aryan course'. Equally naive are the demands of Muslim students that research in areas such as history, sociology, medicine, politics and biology (evolutionary theory) be bound, from the start, to 'given facts' supposedly found in the Qur'an and the Sunnah. This is the wrong track.

The sciences will automatically become Islamic when devout, practicing Muslim scientists produce top results in their fields and when society as such sets its own Islamic priorities after having learned to perceive matters in a Muslim way. At any rate, the dream of the unity of all knowledge cannot replace specialization. Nor can it be realized merely by using a computer to establish a 'universal Islamic data bank' or by digitally analyzing the text of the Qur'an, as at the Institut Alif in Paris.

In short, Islamic science is a science practiced in a scientific spirit and with scientific methods by *Muslim* scientists. Any other definition is mere word fetishism or refers to something else.

Luckily the beginnings of a return to scientific curiosity in the Islamic world, particularly in the field of liberal arts (social sciences), can already be seen. Muslims of European or American origin are naturally playing an important role in this development.[28] Reference should be made here to the extraordinary contribution to Islamic research made by Leopold Weiss (alias Muhammad Asad, 1900–1992).

The dedication in his annotated translation of the Qur'an reads: "To people who think."

---

28. And not only in the sciences but in all fields of Islamic activities, like charity organizations, missionary work, media and civic rights, such as by Yusuf Islam (Cat Stevens), Malcolm X (Malik El-Shabbazz), and Muhammad Ali (Cassius Clay); see the *Autobiography of Malcolm X* by Alex Haley; M. Ali's interview with *Young Muslim*, Chicago, 1997, vol. 2, no. 2; and Steven Barboza, *American Jihad*, N.Y., NY, 1994.

MYSTICISM

Although, compared to orthodox Judaism, Islam has far fewer regulations governing behavior in everyday life, to Western eyes this faith appears to be a 'lawyers' religion,' whose theologians in addition, if not as a matter of priority, have to be legal experts, because Islam tries indeed to shape and regulate the entire course of a believer's day.

This observation is correct, especially when compared to the way a modern Catholic passes his day. Nowadays, he does not encounter a single canonical hurdle from one Sunday mass to the next—the Sunday mass can even be brought forward to Saturday evening if desired. His last ritual duties, to genuinely fast or to receive Communion on an empty stomach, were long ago sacrificed to 'modern rationality'.

By contrast, the life of the Muslim is really structured by Islam from morning until night, not only by the fixed times for ritual prayer, but also by dietary regulations and rules of etiquette. These are not so much based on the Qur'an, which in actual fact only contains three or four dozen binding norms, primarily relating to family and inheritance law. Rather, the Muslim's life is regulated by the Sunnah—the Prophet's exemplary way of conduct.[1] The chapter "Islamic Jurisprudence" explains what this means for areas such as etiquette, which the Westerner would not even consider to be of a legal nature.[2]

It is all the more important that Islam sustains its proper spirituality as 'God's own religion'. This presupposes that Muslims always keep their worship of God alive, free from routine, filling their rituals with an inner life through a process of spiritualization, so that they do not ossify on an exterior level, but in the Benedictine sense rather achieve an equilibrium between action and contemplation, work and prayer.

This inner harmony of people fully oriented to the Afterlife, but with feet planted firmly on the ground of This Life was achieved in the early days of Islam by Muhammad, Abu Bakr, 'Umar, 'Uthman, 'Ali, and quite a few other men and women. They were unreservedly God-fearing, ready

---

1. As illustrated by Ahmad von Denffer, *A Day with the Prophet*, Leicester 1981; Marwan I. Al Kaysī, *Morals and Manner in Islam*, Leicester 1986.

2. Yusuf al Qaradawi, *The Lawful and Unlawful in Islam*, IIFSO, Kuwait 1989. Available also in German and French.

to sacrifice themselves; they were ascetics, practicing the Sufi ideal of 'dying before death'—though without calling or considering themselves mystics.

Keeping God in your mind at all times (*dhikr*) with a pure heart and humility, seeing Him as the most important factor in the shaping of your own life—being a Sufi in this sense—must be the aim of *every* devout Muslim.

But Sufism means something else too: the attempt to acquire knowledge of hidden truths through following a difficult mystical path with the aim of temporarily achieving union with God.

The Naqshabandi brotherhood (which remains within the fold of Sunni Islam) describes the stages of this path in the following way to find successively:

- exterior purity through obeying the law (shari'ah);
- inner union through obeying asceticism (*tarīqah*);
- closeness to God through gnostic knowledge (*ma'rifah*); and
- union with God through reaching the truth (*ḥaqīqah*).[3]

The third and fourth steps on this ladder are problematic, in that they are steps of speculative philosophy, which, incidentally, Jewish and Christian mystics have also tried to ascend. Thus, Nicolas of Cusa, for example, described the aim of mystical theology as 'the union of Yes with No, the overcoming of the Either-Or of all philosophy, and the abandonment of the knowledge of reason in that very darkness in which the impossible becomes visible as the truly necessary'.[4]

The step called *ma'rifah* is problematic since it represents the inappropriate attempt to cross the limits of common knowledge which is based on our sensory perception, the use of reason, and revelation, and to do this in an a-rational (if not irrational) way, namely through 'illumination' in an intuitive or ecstatic manner.

This attempt is understandable as a reaction to the frustration which everyone suffers who is hungry for the truth when, thanks to uncompromising critiques of perception—whether by Kant, Wittgenstein or Popper—he or she grasps that we can comprehend the incomprehensibility of the incomprehensible, but not the incomprehensible itself; that any

---

3. Xavier Jacob, "Derwischorden in der heutigen Türkei," *CIBEDO*, Frankfurt 1990, no. 5/6, pp. 129–157.

4. "Das mystische Paradox," *Neue Zürcher Zeitung*, 28. 4. 1988, p. 41.

honest philosophy must renounce ontology and limit itself to a theory of knowledge.

The Sufi's unwillingness to be content with this kind of *docta ignorantia,* scholarly knowledge of our structural ignorance, is hubris, particularly in view of the warning given in verse 7 of *Sūrat Āl 'Imrān* (3) of the Qur'an:

> **He it is Who has revealed the Book to you: some of its verses are clear in and by themselves—and these are the essence of the Book—and others are allegorical. Now as for those whose hearts are given to swerving from the truth, they pursue the part of it which is allegorical, seeking discord and searching for its hidden meanings. But no one knows its hidden meanings except God.**

This clearly prohibits speculation. It takes into account the fact that divine revelation in the Qur'an had to make use of human speech, that is, a man-made system of communication, which is not suited to the description of metaphysical realities except in a pictorial-allegorical way.

In other words: we are called upon (and well-advised, if we are to avoid nonsensical language games) to forgo any interpretation of metaphysical passages in the Qur'an, just as we should renounce metaphysics in the philosophical field proper.

An example of the kind of *ma'rifah* which emerges from the esoteric path of Islamic mysticism is the fascinating work of the Andalusian Al Shaykh al Akbar, Muḥyi al Dīn Ibn 'Arabi (1165–1240): Islamic Gnosticism, Neoplatonism cloaked in Islamic terms.[5] The most typical examples are his cosmology, eschatology, mysticism of letters and numbers, and his exalted theory of 'The Light of Muhammad'. Here the Prophet of Islam, who rejected all this, is worshiped as God's first creation, in his luminous essence as the sun of existence, as a bearer of all secrets of that which is not manifest, as the archetype of light in the world of ideas.[6]

---

5. As an introduction: Ibn Arabi, *La Profession de Foi,* Paris 1985; Tilman Nagel, "Ibn al 'Arabi und das Asch'aritentum," in *Festschrift für A. Falaturi,* Cologne 1991, pp. 206ff.; Michel Chodkiewicz, *Un Océan sans Rivage,* Paris 1992; English version: *An Ociean without Shore, Ibn 'Arabi, the Book, and the Law,* N.Y., NY 1993 and his *Seal of the Saints—Prophethood and Sainthood in the Doctrine of Ibn 'Arabi,* Cambridge, UK 1993

6. Another Sufi, Frithjof Schuon goes as far as to compare Muhammad with the Logos, without which the world would not have been created; see his, *Den Islam verstehen,* Munich 1988.

Their quest for hidden truths has driven some Muslim sufis into obscurantism: Believing in the magical value of numbers or letters; others became entangled in syncretism in the attempt to understand everything and to love everyone. From Jelaladdin Rumi in medieval Konya[7] to Frithjof Schuon in this century Sufis have taught that all religions are in as much as each of them allows (only) a limited view of reality in its entirety. Thus, following Ibn al 'Arabi, Schuon even accepts the Christian Trinity in its archetypal aspect, namely, as Super-Being, Being and Existence, or Being (Father), Wisdom (Spirit) and Will (Son).

The conviction to be equipped with the capacity to 'access' unlimited transcendental knowledge, thanks to a supersensory direct vision of the invisible, easily leads to élitism, especially since it is impossible to verify or falsify intuitive cosmic knowledge. In many cases such pretension has led to personality cults centered around charismatic Sufi masters. In some cases it has even turned into Messianism.

Calling themselves Shaykh, Pir, Baba, Dede, Celebi or Marabut, those who regarded themselves as 'masters of the spiritual path' and 'men of esoteric truth' (both formulations are from Ibn al 'Arabi) not only attracted qualified disciples under the spell of their auras but many common, gullible people, too. Some of them become so dependent on their spiritual leader that they suffer from withdrawal symptoms when they feel neglected by him—a clear sign of aberration. The many highly revered domed tombs or 'Marabouts' in the Maghrib are evidence of this deviation.

The fourth step referred to above, the step of 'truth,' union, or fusion with God, is even more problematic; it creates the danger of sliding into pantheism. Whoever seeks to express inexpressible truths in antinomies is closer to pantheism that he might think: Everything is God/Nothing is God; Everything is God/God and His creation are one; God does not exist, but neither is He nonexistent.

This form of mysticism reached a sad climax in the Baghdad mystic Husain Manṣūr al Ḥallāj (857–922), a man intoxicated by God, whose mystical poems still move people today.[8] When reading that he said:

With the eye of the heart I see my Lord and say to Him: Who are YOU? he says to me: You!

---

7. A brief introduction may be found in *Dschelaladdin Rumi, Aus dem Diwan*, Stuttgart 1964. Also see *Signs of the Unseen, The Discourses of Jalaluddin Rumi*, trans. W.M. Thackston, Jr., Putney, Vermont 1994.

8. Ḥallaj, *Poèmes mystiques*, Paris 1985.

or

His spirit is my spirit, my spirit His spirit, if he wishes, I wish, and if I wish He wishes.

It is not difficult to see that Ḥallāj was seeking martyrdom, and even provoking his execution for blasphemy. What else could he expect when writing:

I deny the religion of God; this is a duty for me, a sin for Muslims.

Kill me, authorities; for it is my life to be killed, and my death is in my life and my life in my death.

Of course Islamic mysticism does not have to go this far, it does not have to lead to this. What could be called orthodox Sufism is exemplified by the teachings of Shaykh Muhyi al Din 'Abd al Qādir Jilānī,[9] who died in 1166 and is still honored today by people inside as well as outside his Qadirīyah brotherhood. The work of Farīd al Dīn 'Aṭṭar (c. 1136–1220)[10] and Abu Ḥāmid al Ghazālī, the most important 'orthodox' Muslim Sufi (died 1111),[11] testify to Shaykh 'Abd al Qadir's universal acceptance.

At any rate, Sufism does not necessarily mean spirituality. Techniques such as the whirling or wailing of the dervishes named after these practices, even the *dhikr* prayer in the community, based on constant repetition, can degenerate into hypnosis or vulgar spectacle.[12] Discipleship can become slavish obedience.

Some brotherhoods have degenerated into the political maneuvering during periods of decadence. This happened, at the end of the Ottoman empire, amongst the Bektashi in particular, and in the Maghrib during the French occupation. Here it was Moroccan brotherhoods, (*al Wazzānīyah*) above all, who collaborated with the French.

---

9. Abd al Qadir Jilānī, *Futūḥ al Ghaib* (*Enthüllungen des Verborgenen*), Cologne 1985.

10. Bernd Manuel Weischer, *Die nächtlichen Gespräche des Fariduddin 'Attar*, Munich 1981.

11. In addition to his main work—*Ihyā 'Ulūm al Dīn*—reference must here be made to Ghazali's famous *Confessions* and his purely mystical *Mishkāt al Anwār*.

12. A very graphic portrayal of the practice of *dhikr* in present-day Egypt was given by Thomas Ross in the *Frankfurter Allgemeine Zeitung*, 22. 7. 1986, p. 7. I observed *dhikr* sessions of the Halveti-Jerrahi Brotherhood in Istanbul which induced toxic reactions through depriving the body of oxygen. This was achieved by repeated forceful exhalation while pronouncing the last syllable of 'Allahu'.

For all these reasons Sunni orthodoxy, embodied in the figure of Ahmad b. Taymīyah (died 1328), has adopted an attitude which is hostile to Sufis.[13]

Nevertheless, it is evident and should be acknowledged by all that Islamic mysticism has made an indispensible contribution to the increase of piety and the improvement of knowledge about Islam amongst common people. Sufism was not only a counter-weight to the dangers of an all too legalistic religion; it is thanks to Muslim brotherhoods that Islam was able to survive even under extremely hostile conditions, such as in the Central Asian Republics of the former Soviet Union and in Communist Albania.[14]

It is now clear that mystics from all the great religions may be neatly ranked together, be it for their common achievements, be it for their common problematics—Meister Eckhart, John of the Cross, Angelus Silesius, Theresa of Avila alongside Hasan al Basri, al Junaid or Yahya al Suhrawardi.[15]

It would be wrong to believe that Islamic mysticism has no role to play in our rationalistic era. Quite the opposite! The great classical brotherhoods—in particular the Naqshabandīyah, who owned 450 dervish houses(tekke) in Istanbul as late as 1920—are just as alive as younger *turuq* (Sufi brotherhoods). Particularly successful in the spread of Islam in West Africa was the Aḥmadīyah, founded only in the early nineteenth century by the Algerian Ahmad Tijani. Today, with its center in Fes, Morocco, it is the strongest political, economic, and social force in Senegal, before the rival Muridīyah.

It may surprise one to learn that many important Western Muslims, especially in France, have found their way to Islam via mysticism. The most famous among these is probably René Guénon (alias Shaykh 'Abd al Wahid Yahya of the Shadhiliyah brotherhood, 1886-1951), whose work *La Crise du Monde Moderne* had already been published in seven editions by 1946.[16] In England, it is Martin Lings (alias Abu Bakr

13. See Henri Laoust, *La profession de foi d'Ibn Taymiyya—La Wasifīya*, Paris 1986.

14. A good overview is to be found in Annemarie Schimmel, *Mystical Dimensions of Islam*, London, 1975.

15. See Kurt Ruh, *Geschichte der abendländischen Mystik*, Munich 1990ff; Geofffrey Parrinder, *Mysticism in the World's Religions*, Rockport, MA 1995.

16. René Guénon, *La Crise du Monde moderne*, Paris 1981, edited in English as *Crisis of the Modern World*.

Sirajuddin) who was shown this path by the Algerian Shaykh al 'Alawī.[17] Among these Europeans there are those—such as Charles-André Gilis— who give themselves up to uninhibited, unlimited speculation,[18] in the face of which one can only admire how much some of our contemporaries seem to know of God and His creation.

Idries Shah's Sufi books can now be found in the esoteric section of every bookshop; and Sufi brotherhood music is found in every good record shop.[19]

Islam is, however, far from being alone in this renewed interest in the mystical. Cabbalistic Hassidism is flourishing in New York no less than in Jerusalem. And the groundswell of charismatic 'grassroots' churches in the Christian world is heading towards mysticism as well.

Background to this trend is increasing doubt, not only in rationality as an exclusive method, but also in the rationality of the Western scientific and social system: a system which has led to the two World Wars, Stalinism, the employment of nuclear weapons, environmental disaster, and underdevelopment: A system which did not even prevent the Holocaust. The current young generation has exposed the ideology of progress espoused by the so-called 1968 generation to be pure pathos.

Modern micro- and macrophysics prepared the ground for this rebellion against scientism when, at the beginning of the present century, this sci- ence—whose key words are 'quantum theory' and 'the uncertainty prin- ciple'—first moved beyond classical physics and then came up against fresh systematic limits to the expansion of knowledge, and, indeed, the mystical.[20]

At any rate, one gets the impression that many young people want to correct rationalistic blunders by embarking on another course equally bound to fail—the escape into irrationality, with total surrender to new myths, following the motto: "It is so nice to obey blindly!"[21]

17. See Martin Lings, *A Sufi Saint of the Twentieth Century: Shaykh Ahmad al Alawi*, Cambridge, UK 1993; Johan Cartigny, *Cheikh al Alawi*, Paris 1984. He lived in Mostaganem (Algeria) earlier this century.

18. See, for example, Charles-André Gilis, *Marie en Islam*, Paris 1990.

19. See Alfons Hirth, "Musik der . . . Sufi-Bruderschaften," in *Fono-Forum* 4/1991; of Idries' many works we refer only to *The Sufis* (1964).

20. It is worth while reading Gaston Bachelard, *Le Nouvel Esprit Scientifique*, Paris 1934; Henri Atlan, *A tort et à raison—Intercritique de la science et du mythe*, Paris 1986; Hans-Peter Dürr (ed), *Physik und Transzendenz*, Berne 1989.

21. Marcel Reich-Ranicki, "Es ist so schön, sich zu fügen, Hinwendung zum Mystizismus—ein Generationsproblem," *Frankfurter Allgemeine Zeitung*—supplement to no. 248 of 25. 10. 1986.

Eugen Biser sees another mechanism behind this: modern man's abolition of sin, among other things, through 'structural exculpation'. One useful method of such exculpation is the adoption of personal convictions as
a moral standard *(Gesinnungsethik)*, as if good intentions could sanctify
the methods and results of any action. But despite this modern man still
fails to achieve his 'salvation'. In fact, as it turns out, he has only replaced
his earlier problem of guilt with his new problem of suffering from the
meaninglessness of his existence. In turn, this has led to the current 'religious proliferation' with its anti-intellectual attitude, i.e., a tendency
towards fundamentalism and/or mysticism. According to Karl Rahner, we
may extrapolate from all this that "the Christian of the future will be a
mystic or not at all."[22] I believe that the issue is somewhat different: can
a mystic, equipped with the Neoplatonic theory of ontological oneness
and the Neoplatonic emanation theory, remain in any sense a believer in
the Trinity and the Christian concept of creation?

At any rate, alongside Rahner's alternatives there is a third logical
option: to become a Muslim, thereby marrying rationality with the non-
sensual reality.

---

22. Eugen Biser, "Fundamentalismus und Mystik: Christentum im Widerspruch der
Gegenwart," *Die Presse*, Vienna, 18/19. 3. 1989.

FATALISM

The relevant entry in *The Columbia Encyclopedia* states that Islam "teaches an absolute predestination." In fact, Westerners almost universally believe that Islam is fatalistic.

The stereotype media image of the Muslim who has quietly surrendered to his fate, regarding everything as *kismet* or *maktūb,* and who sits in weary resignation in front of his hut, motionless, squinting into the sun, is quite popular. But it perpetuates a misconception.

True, however, is that Muslims have remained uncommonly conscious of the problems associated with the concepts of 'predestination' and 'free will'. Christianity is also essentially deterministic with its doctrine of original sin, but if anything, it has marginalized the entire issue—as if it could escape coping with it.

On the basis of their (in this respect identical) image of God, the fundamental and highly troubling question arises in both religions of how God's omnipotence and omniscience may be logically reconciled with man's responsibility for his own actions, that is to say, with man's free will (*arbitrium liberum*).

The dilemma is as follows:

Either God is the cause of all action; in which case, man is not responsible for his deeds, and it would contradict divine justice to punish him;

Or man is the cause of his own action; in which case, God is not Creator and Lord of all that happens.

For a long time Christianity tried hard to resolve this dilemma. With its doctrine of grace, e.g., salvation by God's 'eternal choice'—or not at all—it tended, with Augustine, Zwingli, Calvin and the Jansenists of the seventeenth and eighteenth century, towards a radical concept of predestination. Thomas Aquinas, too, whose scholasticism became orthodoxy itself, considered God as the cause of all events. He maintained, however, that His foreknowledge did not imply the inevitability of the concrete course of events. Rather, he suggested that man's free will, as concretely manifested in history, was 'integrated' into God's overall plan of salvation.

But this terminological game could not solve the problem. It merely reformulated it in a way which flattered human experience and ambition. The problem of predestination was even more radically 'solved' in Europe and North America after the Enlightenment. Since then, the virtually absolute freedom of choice, as postulated by the 'autonomous individual,' was accepted as plausible, simply because it corresponded to the masses' new awareness of liberty and freedom. Free will is 'experienced' and no longer questioned. It is regarded as obscurantism if one wonders whether there was not at least some limited form of predetermination—if only by our genes—despite the fact that free will, like its opposite, cannot be scientifically proved. (In the absence of God, of course, theological problems disappear all by themselves.)

In Islam, too, there have been, and still are, various attempts to solve the problem of predestination logically.

In contrast to the belief in complete predestination (held by the *Jabrīyah* school), which manifested itself at an early period of Islam, the *Mu'tazilah* school of philosophy taught free will in Baghdad as early as the ninth century. According to this school, God created the latent ability in man to be a cause of actions. Thus, human action had two causes: one which could be attributed to God, the other to man. It is not in the least surprising that such positions should be revived in the modern era by modernists such as al Afghani (1839–1897)[1] or contemporary neo-Mu'tazilites.

A truly Islamic examination of the question of free will requires a closer examination of the Qur'an and is, therefore, more complex. It takes as a starting-point the image of God, derived from His description of Himself. As is well known, God's 'most beautiful names' (7:180) are (mostly) taken from the Qur'an,[2] and are said to number 99.[3] (The most important name, i.e., attribute, is not among them because it transcends human understanding.) Names refer to essential characteristics—and on no account to persons: They describe aspects, or facets of God and ways in which He manifests Himself. Thus we get to know Him as

• the All-Knowing (*al 'Ālim, al Khabīr, al Muhīt, al Muhsī, al Hasīb, al Samī', al Basīr, al Mudrik*) Who knows everything;

---

1. See p. 49 ff. in Arnold Hottinger, *Allah heute*, Zurich 1981.

2. Daniel Gimaret, *Les noms divins en Islam*, Paris 1988; Abu Hamid al Ghazali, *Ihyā 'Ulūm al Dīn*, Vol. 1, Book 2 of the *The Foundations of the Articles of Faith* series, Lahore 1974.

3. *Sahīh Muslim*, Ch. 1117, hadith no. 6475.

• the Almighty (al Qādir, al Qawī, al Qāhir, al Ghālib, al 'Azīz, al Jabbār);

• the Creator ex nihilo and Preserver of all things (al Khāliq, al Bāri', al Muṣawwir, al Jā'il, al Ṣāni', al Mūjid), i.e., the original cause of everything (al Fā'il, al 'Āmil, al Mubdi');

• the absolute Ruler and Master of everything (al Malik, al Rabb, al Ṣamad);

• the Punisher (al Muntaqim);

• the Just (al 'Ādil, al Ḥākam);

• the Kindly, the Mild One, the Forgiving, the Merciful (al Raḥmān, al Raḥīm, al Muḥsin, al Mutafaḍḍil, al Laṭīf, al Ghaffār, al Ṭawwāb), the Protector and Friend of the believer (al Walī, al Mawla), the Fountain of Love (11:90); the Loving (85:14, 3:31 and 5:54).

This utterly complex image of God highlights the difficulties with the problem of predestination outlined above, a problem mirrored in seemingly contradictory statements throughout the Qur'an.

On the one hand there are dozens of Qur'anic verses from which we may conclude that God—closer to the believer than his jugular vein (50:16)—is the Lord of all events. As al Ghazali said in the twelfth century, "He knows the crawling of the ant on a rock in the darkest night . . . . What He wills is, and what He does not will is not . . . . No one can reject His fate."[4] This point of view can be found in verses such as the following:

And whomsoever God wishes to guide, He expands his breast for Islam, and whom He wishes to go astray, He makes his breast tight and narrow . . . thus does God inflict horror on those who will not believe. (6:125)

God has set a seal upon their hearts and upon their hearing. (2:7)

Yet if We had so willed, We would certainly have imposed Our guidance upon every human being. (32:13)

And certainly We have destined for hell many of the . . . men. (7:179)

---

4. See his "Confession of faith," in Hottinger, op. cit., p. 26; and also his Iḥyā' 'Ulūm al Dīn, op. cit., section 4.

He cannot be questioned concerning what He does, whereas they shall be questioned. (21: 23)

Reading such verses out of context it is possible to reach the conclusion that Allah is an arbitrary God who "**chastises whom He wills**" (3:129), regardless of whether people deserve it, and that all this is eternally fixed.

Yet the Qur'an contains just as many verses which seem to say exactly the opposite, and which are the basis for the moral teachings of Islam. These include:

But as for him who believes and does good, he shall have goodly reward . . .' (18:88)

God would never lead a people astray after He has guided them . . . (9:115)

Say: If I err, I err only due to my own self . . . (34:50).

In view of such widely diverging statements the overriding tendency within Islam since the tenth century has been that, from a human standpoint, there is a dichotomy regarding the nature of God. The question of free will or predestination, which cannot be solved by means of human logic, is a dichotomy which we must simply put up with, despite the perplexities associated with it.

This position was formulated by the anti-Mu'tazilite, Ash'arite school of philosophy and expressed in the traditional 'confession of faith' of Abu al Hasan al Ash'ari (874–935).[5] He called for the acceptance of such mysteries of faith as revealed, without asking 'how' and without seeking comparisons in the human domain (*bilā kayf wa bilā tashbīh*). The greatest Egyptian reformist theologian of our century, Muhammad 'Abdu, adhered to this in his chief work *Risālat al Tawḥīd* (1897): "The attempt to reconcile the Omniscience of God and His Will . . . with man's freedom to act is an attempt to penetrate the secrets of God."[6]

This approach, which appears almost agnostic in its humility, has the Sunnah of the Prophet on its side. He expressly warned against hair-splitting theological speculation—particularly on this subject.[7]

---

5. See Hottinger, *op. cit.*, p. 17 f.

6. Muhammad Abdou, *Rissālat al Tawḥīd*, Paris 1984, p. 43; similarly Hamidullah, *Der Islam*, Geneva 1968, para 121.

7. *Ṣaḥīḥ Muslim*, Ch 1113, Hadith no. 6450.

If we look closer, however, neither al Ash'ari nor al Ghazali nor Muhammad 'Abdu adhered to their epistemological doctrine. All three actually made a vain attempt to reconcile free will with God's Omnipotence in a logical and conceptual way. Al Ash'ari's notion of 'acquisition' (*kasb/iktisāb*) was epoch-making. According to this concept God is the only cause or creator of all human actions, but man can 'acquire' merit (or the opposite) from his deeds. To quote al Ash'ari: "The true meaning of acquisition is the occurrence of an event or a thing due to derived power; for the person by whose derived power it occurs, it is an acquisition." He probably meant by this that, in reality, God alone is the agent in human action, and determines the outcome, but that a person can earn merit or guilt through the mental attitude accompanying the action.[8] If so al Ash'ari simply pushed the issue into the psychological field, opening up the question—again unanswerable—of whether man is free to adopt a mental attitude or not.

Al Ghazali took this concept and, in my view, pushed it a little further in the direction of free will.

> God, the only cause of the action of His creatures, does not prevent them from accomplishing willful actions through acquisition (*al maqdurah*); for God created will (*al qudrah*) and that which is willed (*al maqdūr*), the ability to choose as well as that which is chosen. . . . How can acquired actions be completely attributed to inevitability (*al jabr*), when everyone instinctively understands the difference between voluntary and involuntary (*al ḍarūri*) reflexes?[9]

This, then, is the result of Muslim attempts to come to terms intellectually with the paradox of predestination, without obscuring parts of the admittedly ambivalent, revelation and without exaggerating in either of the two possible directions. If nothing else, then, Muslims have at least developed a greater consciousness of the problem. It is one thing to be unable to solve a problem and quite another to sweep it under the carpet.

Surprisingly, this stance has been rehabilitated by the findings of modern physics. As has been well known since Werner Heisenberg's discovery of the uncertainty principle in 1925, physics has learned to describe

---

8. For details see Majid Fakhry, *A History of Islamic Philosophy*, London 1983, p. 208; and M. Abdul Hye, "Ash'arism," in M. M. Sharif, *A History of Muslim Philosophy*, Wiesbaden 1963, p. 220ff, esp. pp. 229f.

9. See footnote 4, *loc. cit.*, pp. 78f; 'Al Afghani', in Hottinger, *op. cit.*, pp. 49ff. agreed with him.

inner-atomic reality not using alternative but *complementary* states (particles versus waves). It was discovered that particle physics can be better grasped using the Islamic theory of predestination, i.e., its concept of simultaneously determined and undetermined behavior. And, by the same token, Muslims—as Ulrich Schoen has shown—can point out that their own attempts to explain a theological and scientific problem (the problem of causality as a part of the problem of predestination) can no longer be belittled as medieval obscurantist nonsense.[10]

What does this mean in Muslim practice?

Like the Christian and the practicing Marxist (who, if he takes his historical materialism seriously, should actually be a fatalist), the Muslim attempts to achieve his aims in life according to the motto: "Help yourself and God will help you."

He feels personal responsibility for his actions and his omissions. He trusts that God will reward him for his good deeds—not because God is obliged to, but because He denies Himself injustice.[11] The Muslim fears punishment for bad deeds, although he knows of God's mercy and readiness to forgive. Because he is aware that at the end of the day everything is in God's hands, he begins every deed in His name—*bismi-lLāhi!* (in the name of God)—leaving success up to Him—*in sha'a Allah!* (if God is willing)—and attributing every success to Him—*ma sha'a Allah* (as God wishes/wished). Thus he feels protected by the Providence of God, to whom he will, of course, return at the end of his days (10:40).

Only if a Muslim suffers misfortune or if, despite all his attempts a project fails, does his *kismet* attitude come to the fore; he will not despair, will not tear out his hair or rip his clothes, but will recognize and accept that what has happened was *maktūb* (preordained).

And no one ... has his life lengthened nor ... diminished ..., but it is all in a book. (35:11)

As Muhammad Asad observed, Islamic 'fatalism' does not refer to the *future,* but to that which has already occurred, to the past.

---

10. Ulrich Schoen, *Determination und Freiheit im arabischen Denken heute,* Göttingen, 1976; see also Hans-Peter Dürr (ed.) *Physik und Transzendenz,* Berne 1986.
11. *Vierzig Heilige Hadite,* Munich 1987 (translated by A. von Denffer), Hadith no. 17.

FUNDAMENTALISM

Every religion and ideology develops from a basis—the Bible, the Gospels or the writings of Marx, Engels and Lenin, etc.—upon foundations which are regarded as precise, complete, unalterable and sufficient. Islam is no different. Its foundations are 'Qur'an and Sunnah'.

All religions and ideologies also have in common the fact that they develop as a result of their confrontation with specific challenges that differ in space and time.

Thus, increasingly complex systems of ideas and doctrines emerge and finally congeal, during the 'classical' period, into 'orthodoxy'. At this point orthodoxy becomes the politically correct example to follow. The simple believer, comrade or brother is no longer in a position to form his own opinion in view of the complexity of the creed, whose ramifications are no longer accessible to him. When this state of affairs is reached, religion and ideology become the domain of scholars, priests, and ideologues.

Because of this, in all religions and ideologies, from time to time, the need is felt to return to the original belief, to rediscover its foundations, in the hope that the old religion, freed of human ballast, can be revitalized and viewed with fresh eyes, so as to become newly significant for the solution of contemporary problems. Believers become 'Protestant,' attempt to find the 'young Marx', up-date Martin Luther's opponent, Thomas Müntzer or, like the self-styled Christian Franz Alt, try to project a new image of Jesus.

This—and nothing else—deserves the name 'fundamentalism'. Fundamentalists, unlike liberal Jews, are not concerned with a revisionist adaptation of religious foundations to modern requirements. They are not—unlike the Old Catholics and the Society of St. Pius X of the late Bishop Lefèbvre—seeking restoration; rather, their aim is to revitalize the original belief by returning to its sources (*tajdīd, iṣlāḥ*).

This endeavor may take the path of a 'rational fundamentalism' which, while proceeding from the exact wording of the revelation seeks to distill its guiding principles, its timeless rationale. Or it may take the path of a (certainly not irrational) 'literary fundamentalism,' concerned primarily with returning to the text of the revelation which alone, and absolutely, is to be taken seriously, and literally so, word by word.

The first tendency aspires to a return to the source without methodical limitations, the second exclusively by way of establishing the authentic wording of the sources. The former wants to reinterpret them constructively, the second not at all.

Both types of fundamentalism are found in Islam. However, the term 'fundamentalism' has no true Arabic equivalent.[1] It is a Western creation, coined to describe a Western phenomenon.

In the narrower sense of 'literary' fundamentalism the term was, in fact, first coined for American evangelical Christians, who, in the nineteenth century seriously attempted a purely literal understanding and application of the Bible and who, above all as 'Creationists,' rejected the vulgarized evolutionary theory developed from Darwin.[2]

The same term can also be applied to Jews like Rabbi Menachem Schneerson's Hassidic 'Lubavites' in New York or their spiritual cousins in Jerusalem, when they indulge in a narrowly literal understanding of the Bible without compromise.

Fundamentalism is not, then, an Islamic phenomenon. It has always been around, in both senses of the word. It may be defined as 'an attitude to and view of the world or, in a narrower sense, a movement which takes the legal norms, values and behavioral patterns of the earliest period of Islam as absolute model for the shaping of the present.'[3]

Since the tenth century the Ḥanbali school of law, together with the epistemological philosophy of the Ash'arites, has been a strong influence on Sunni Islam in the form of a fundamentalism which seems to allow literal understanding alone.

Shaykh Wali Allah (died 1763), Muhammad b. 'Abd al Wahhab, the founder of Wahhabism (died 1787), Muhammad b. Ali al Sanūsī, founder of the Sanūsī movement in Libya (died 1860),[4] the organization of

---

1. To describe the phenomenon, Arabs have belatedly created the term *al 'uṣulīyah* (concern with the sources).

2. See Henry M. Morris, *Scientific Creationism,* San Diego 1974; Wolfgang Klauswitz, "Mensch und Dinosaurier—Der Kampf der amerikanischen Creationisten gegen die Evolution," *Frankfurter Allgemeine Zeitung,* 7 November 1986. The Muslim world is affected to a lesser extent by this because Darwinism has never been a universally accepted dogma there. Muslims admit that God may create by a process of programmed evolution.

3. This definition was formulated during a colloquium on Islam held on 22 January 1987 in the German Foreign Office.

4. See Knut S. Vikor, *Sufi and Scholar on the Desert Edge: Muhammad Ibn Ali al Sanusi and his Brotherhood,* C. Hurst & Co., London 1995.

Egyptian Muslim brothers, and the Pakistani Jamaat-i-Islami have all revived this approach.

Then, as now, literary fundamentalists were denigrated as naive, if not stupid for their supposedly primitive literalism. And yet their approach corresponds to the attitude of modern analytical philosophy (of language) toward metaphysics.

Current textual analysis of the New Testament underscores the precarious nature of these texts, thus accelerating de-Christianization. The equivalent analysis of the Qur'an, carried out as meticulously by Western Orientalists has, on the contrary, fully substantiated both the authenticity of this text and its astounding compatibility with contemporary scientific research.[5]

Nevertheless, Islam has to cope with the very same semantic problems which even the very simplest linguistic text poses: how is the Qur'an to be understood, particularly in passages which are ambiguous, downright puzzling or clearly allegorical?

Allegories are more than pictorial paraphrases if they refer, not to sensorily perceptible facts, but to metaphysical reality—the transcendental— because statements of an ontological nature, including the existence and essence of God, *ipso facto* escape direct experience.

In that case, allegories unavoidably present codes, which cannot be deciphered, let alone analyzed: Communications whose message we can only make out like shadows behind a veil and which we can only 'understand' in our anthropological way. For, in as much as metaphysical truth eludes our perception, it also eludes language communication (since that, too, rests on perception).

Thus, when a prophet announces metaphysical realities he engages in the transmission of what is the unsayable.

This should have been understood, not only by literary fundamentalists but by all Muslims, ever since Fritz Mauthner (1849–1923), Gottlob Frege (1848–1925)—with his essay "Über Sinn und Bedeutung (On Sense and Meaning)" (1892)—and Ludwig Wittgenstein (1889–1951) used their critique of language to demonstrate the unsuitability of any language for metaphysical discourse.[6]

---

5. See Maurice Bucaille, *The Bible, the Qur'an and Science: The Holy Scriptures Examined in the Light of Modern Knowledge*, translated by Alastair D. Pannell and Maurice Bucaille, Indianapolis, 1978.

6. See Fritz Mauthner, *Wörterbuch der Philosophie*, 2 vols, Zurich 1980; Ludwig Wittgenstein, *Tractatus logico-philosophicus*, Frankfurt 1963; Wittgenstein, *Philosophische Untersuchungen*, Frankfurt 1971.

All Muslims should be aware that the attempt to clarify metaphysical allegories in the Qur'an—to which, to be sure, even the word 'Allah' belongs—via 'logical,' reasoned interpretations, leads to the same intellectual thin-ice, i.e., self-deceptive linguistic games, as did the ontological speculations of classical philosophy.

Therefore, consciously or unconsciously, along with the entire Qur'an, literary Islamic fundamentalists take verse 7 of *Surat Āl 'Imrān* (3) literally:

> **Some of its verses are clear in and by themselves—and these are the essence of the Book—and others are allegorical . . . but no one knows its final meaning except God.**

Literal-minded fundamentalists heed this by humbly and intelligently renouncing metaphysics, theology, and mysticism.

If it is a sign of intelligence to accept the narrow limits of human perception and logic in the wake of Kant and Wittgenstein, why should it be a sign of stupidity when Muslims do the same with regard to metaphysical statements in the Qur'an?

In his dealings with the revealed text the literary fundamentalist is a believing skeptic, a skeptical nominalist who has the Qur'an on his side:

> **But most of them follow nothing but conjecture; surely conjecture will never be a substitute for truth.(10:36)[7]**

'Rational fundamentalism,' on the other hand, began in modern times at the end of the nineteenth and beginning of the twentieth century with the *Salafiyah* reform movement (literally: 'going back to the past, emulating the example of the ancients'). It was developed by figures such as Muhammad 'Abdu,[8] Rashid Rida,[9] Shaykhs Ibn Badis, al Ibrahimi, and Muhammad Asad.[10] Theirs was a reaction to the paralysis and decadence of the Islamic world of the time[11] and its progressive dependence on the West, a reaction which, however, often remained painfully apologetic.

---

7. See also Qur'an 5:101 and 42:10, verses which also advise modesty in interpretation.

8. Muhammad 'Abdu, *Risālat al Tawḥīd*, Paris 1984, was a milestone.

9. Muhammad Rashid Riḍā (1865-1935) edited Abdu's revolutionary commentary of the Qur'an after his death which was later published as *Tafsīr al Manār*.

10. Muhammad Asad (1900–1992) demonstrates *salafiyah* in his translation of the Qur'an, *The Message of the Qur'an*, Gibraltar 1980.

11. The depressing situation which ruled in Makkah in the nineteenth century has been portrayed by Johann Ludwig Burckhardt, *In Mekka und Medina*, Weimar 1830; Richard

As causes of the decline of the Muslim world the *Salafiyah* identified the half-heartedness and laxity of belief of a timid *Ummah* and, above all, the disastrous medieval notion of 'closing the door to interpretation' (*taqlid*)—the idea that everything worth knowing is already known, available in the Qur'an and Sunnah, and that, in comparison to the early Muslims, later Muslims suffered an unbridgeable disadvantage when trying to understand the divine message.

Unfortunately, in the Middle Ages, triumphalist conclusions have been drawn from the concluding revelation:

> **This day have I perfected your religion for you and completed My favor on you . . . (5:3)**

In opposition to these notions, the Salafite reformers demanded that the door be re-opened for efforts towards a modern understanding of Islam (*ijtihad*).

At the same time, the *Salafiyah* were attempting to cleanse their religion from non-Islamic elements which had infiltrated over time—superstitions, in particular, in the form of worshipping graves and saints (*maraboutism*), Sufi aberrations, and heretic elements.

But the reformers saw a revival of Islam as possible only if, together with the sacrifice of many medieval glosses and casuistry, a clear distinction was made between the true sources of Islam: The Qur'an and the authentic Sunnah of the Prophet (and *only* the Prophet) on the one hand, and the marvelous edifice of Islamic jurisprudence and scholarship, on the other—the latter being the result of human efforts, and therefore fallible, as specific responses to specific problems. Correspondingly, a conceptual difference was made between Shari'ah as pure Qur'anic divine law and Fiqh as norms derived from it through human efforts, and not *ipso facto* eternally binding law.[12]

This was revolutionary. The Muslims were supposed to reaccustom themselves to the idea (familiar to early Islam) that the Qur'an does not regulate everything, but only those things which God thinks necessary to regulate; that there are areas of activity left to human regulation, and also areas which must not be limited by any human regulation whatsoever.

F. Burton, *Personal Narrative of a Pilgrimage to Al Madinah & Meccah*, 2 vols., London 1864; Heinrich von Maltzan, *Meine Wallfahrt nach Mekka, 1865*, Tübingen 1982.

12. See Muhammad Asad, *This Law of Ours*, Gibraltar 1987.

This new approach to the sources by no means signifies an adaptation of the Qur'an to the *zeitgeist,* but, on the contrary, signals the recovery of the flexibility the Holy Book guarantees, not only in its spirit, but literally too, for the solution of problems as they emerge through the course of history.

Unfortunately, with their methods, the fathers of the *Salafiyah* did not succeed in developing a convincing model for the Islamic State and Islamic economics.[13] Being the product of an education system that aimed at the preservation of heritage through learning by heart, they were probably still too timid. Even so they did help to reform the education system itself; for example, Shaykh 'Abdu greatly advanced al Azhar University in Cairo.

In any case, the fathers of rational fundamentalism were too pious and conscientious to chop their way through 1400 years of Islamic scholarship. They made the right to fresh interpretation dependent on the following qualifications:

- Since the Qur'an was revealed in the Arab dialect of the Quraysh, knowledge of that vernacular and of the understanding of the Prophet and early Islam is indispensable for a contemporary understanding of the Qur'an;
- this presupposes mastery of the history of the Prophet *(sīrah)* and of the Hadith sciences; and
- all earlier commentaries of the Qur'an must be analyzed as to their continued relevance, i.e., nothing must be rejected off hand.

It is hardly surprising that someone who has mastered all these areas of knowledge—from Arabic grammar to pre-Islamic lyrics—is hardly prone to be innovative. The door to interpretation is open for him, yes, but he is unlikely to cross its threshold. This is why, even today—from Madinah to Fes—the typical Islamic scholar is still very similar to his medieval counterpart, despite the *Salafiyah*. The typical *'alim* still only knows Arabic and has deplorable knowledge of the non-Islamic world.

However, since the 1970s the scene has changed. As Gilles Kepel[14] has outlined, rational fundamentalism today is represented and promoted less

---

13. But Muhammad Asad has done well with his *The Principles of State and Government in Islam (1961),* Gibraltar 1980.

14. Kepel, Gilles, *Intellectuels et militants de l'Islam contemporain,* Paris 1990; also see his *The Revenge of God: The Resurgence of Islam, Christianity and Judaism in the Modern World,* Oxford 1994.

by a reforming 'clergy' than by scientific and technical Muslim intelligentsia. It is possible to witness the phenomenon in almost all Islamic
countries where it is not students of the humanities, but of engineering who
are now providing the impetus for political change and re-Islamization.
This is an intelligentsia educated, if not in Western universities, then
according to Western methods, but who remain bound to Islam in an ethical and moral sense.

With few inhibitions, these people read the Qur'an almost naively, at
any rate unburdened by profound theological knowledge. They read the
word of God without a filter and very selectively extract from it individual passages which seem to be of great and immediate significance for
them personally. The associated danger of radicalism and politicization—
always the privilege of the young—is obvious. This is especially true if
students seek, but do not find a justification in the Qur'an for the existence of kings and single party regimes.

If there is a danger for the stability of Muslim States today then it
comes more from this enthusiastic form of fundamentalism than the frequently less intellectual Islamic integrism, to which a later chapter is dedicated.[15]

---

15. In the meantime, fundamentalism has almost been studied to death. Book titles and
articles carrying this term go into thousands. Most ambitious, however, is the
Fundamentalist Project of the American Academy of Arts and Sciences—four volumes
with over 3000 pages, called *Fundamentalism Observed*—appearing since 1991.

TOLERANCE OR VIOLENCE?

The assertion that Islam is the religion of tolerance *par excellence* often seems preposterous to Western observers. And yet it is true.

The Qur'an repeatedly maintains that differences between men, in terms of color, wealth, race, and language, are natural (30:22); Allah even describes ideological and religious pluralism as God-given:

> ... and if God had so willed, surely He could have made you one single community, but (He willed otherwise) in order to test you by what He gave you. Therefore, compete with one another in all virtues. (5:48)

This basic pluralism is the antithesis of the Catholic doctrine of *extra ecclesiam nullum salus*. The Prophet of Islam even predicted that his own community would split into many groups,[1] indulging in excessive pluralism.

That this attitude compels tolerance is corroborated in other verses of the Qur'an:

> And say: The truth is from your Lord, so let him who so pleases believe in it, and let him who so pleases reject it. (18:29)

> And if your Lord had so willed, surely all those who live on earth would have believed, all of them. Will you then compel men to believe? (10:99)

Thus it is clear that Islam does not sanction the kind of aggressive preaching practiced by some Christian missionary orders. Even the Prophet was warned against this:

> You are only a warner ... (11:12)

---

1. *Sunan Abū Dāwud*, ḥadith no. 4596, *Sunan al Tirmidhi*, ḥadith no. 2640,*Sunan Ibn Majah*, hadith no. 3991, and *Musnad Ahmad Ibn Hanbal* 2/332.

> And ask those who have received revelation and the uninstructed
> people: "Do you submit yourselves ?" And if they submit to Him,
> then indeed they follow the right way; but if they turn away, then
> your duty is only to deliver the message. (3:20)

> Say: "O you people! Now the truth from your Lord has come to
> you, therefore, whoever chooses the right path, follows it only for
> his own good, and whoever chooses to go astray, goes astray only to
> his own loss. And I am not responsible for you." (10:108)

At the heart of this attitude of comprehensive intellectual and practical
tolerance is the fundamental statement in 2:256, a statement both factual
and normative:

There is no compulsion in matters of faith.

This means that since faith concerns the *forum internum,* religious compulsion is a futile attempt; indeed, it is forbidden even to undertake such
a hopeless venture.

For this reason religious disputes should be carried out in a friendly and
peaceful manner, and their outcome left to God (4:59).

In almost every *surah,* the Qur'an encourages man to contemplate, to
use his powers of reason, to harvest the fruit of his thought, instead of
simply repeating authorities parrot fashion.

But what if a Muslim should thereby lose his faith and become a renegade ?

Islam even passes this test of tolerance, despite the fact that apostasy
has time and again been punished with the death penalty, not only during
the Middle Ages, but as late as our own century in the Sudan.[2]

This came about through the untenable equating of peaceful desertion
from the faith (*riddah*) with the criminal act of high treason by actively
fighting one's earlier faith, Islam.

---

2. The septuagenarian Sudanese theologian Mahmud Muhammad Taha was executed
in January 18, 1985 under Head of State Ja'far Numeiri for apostasy, amongst other things
for his differentiation of eternally valid and no longer valid regulations in the Qur'an.

At any rate the voice of reason rules this matter today, represented by personalities such as Muhammad Asad[3] and Fathi Osman, who judged the execution of Taha Mahmud Taha as unreservedly un-Islamic.[4]

That is the theory. But what about Islamic tolerance in practice?

What about the Palestinian Arab terrorists, who attack jets, cruise liners and airports? What about G.I.A. guerrillas slashing throats in Algeria?

Of course the phenomenon of political terrorism, religiously colored, exists in many regions of the world. But this has nothing to do with Islam or any other religion. At least no more than the violence of non-Muslims, also on the point of despair, has to do with Christianity: supporters of 'liberation theology' in South America,[5] Northern Irish urban guerrillas, members of the German 'Red Army Faction,' the French 'Action Directe,' and of the Italian 'Brigate Rosse'.[6]

And yet, leaving violence aside, there is also the phenomenon of lower key intolerance among Muslims which we must face.

Is it not true that public eating, drinking or smoking during Ramadan is punishable by imprisonment in Morocco? Is it not true that the religious police in Saudi Arabia check up on whether people are praying at the right time? Did Algerian Muslims not physically enforce the prohibition of alcohol and the head covering for women? Is it not true that in the Islamic world there is fear of a 'period of feverish, rigorous, word fetishist intolerance?'[7]

Of course, this too has a theoretical and a practical background.

Here the fact is important that the fundamental command of tolerance in *Sūrat al Baqarah* (2), verse 256, was revealed in the context of

---

3. See Muh. Asad, *The Message of the Qur'an*, Gibraltar 1980, footnote 45 to 5:33, but also Muh. Hamidullah, *Der Islam*, Geneva 1968, para 440.

4. Fathi Osman, "Islam and the freedom of faith," *ARABIA*, London, June 1985, p. 10 and November 1985, p. 11; Osman, *The Children of Adam. An Islamic Perspective on Pluralism*, Washington, DC 1996.

5. It was already made clear, in an instruction from the Vatican on the subject in 1984, that the Catholic Church was becoming worried about the tendencies to violence in the area of 'liberation theology'. In a subsequent "Instruction on Christian freedom and liberation" in 1986 its doctrinal congregation condemned "the systematic recourse to violence allegedly necessary for liberation" and prohibited Christian activists from having anything to do with terrorism; see also Martin Kriele, "Die linksfaschistische Häresie," *Frankfurter Allgemeine Zeitung*, 28 May 1986, p. 11.

6. See Thomas Ross, "Mit teuflisch gutem Gewissen," *Frankfurter Allgemeine Zeitung*, 12 July 1985.

7. Slimane Zeghidour, "La fin de l'islam débonnaire," in *Le Matin du Sahara et du Maghrib*, Casablanca 24 February 1991, pp. 8 f.

Muslim relations with the outside world, i.e., the relations between Islam and the other scriptural religions.

This is why many of today's young Muslims, in their conduct towards fellow believers, focus on another principle, found in eight more or less identical statements in the Qur'an.[8] Accordingly, believers may be recognized by the fact that they "command what is right" (*al amru bi al ma'rūf*) and "prohibit what is wrong" (*al anhyi 'an al munkār*). In accordance with the Sunnah, the Muslim should do this "with his hand" if possible, otherwise "with his tongue," and if this is impossible, then at least "with his heart."[9]

It is clear that the application of this instruction, taken out of context, can make Muslims who should be 'guardians of virtue,' spies and 'vigilantes,' a people who take the execution of justice, law and order into their own hands, taking on simultaneously the responsibilities of prosecutor, judge and executioner.

Those who think or, worse, act in this way may violate the following seven fundamental principles of Islam:

1. The Qur'an has institutionalized government (by an *amīr*) and, therefore, the Islamic State. This implies that in Islam, too, the exercise of power is a government monopoly. As soon as the State is in a position to impose a prohibition of alcohol, the individual Muslim is not allowed to take his axe to the bar.

2. Compulsion in matters of religion breeds hypocrisy, an attitude which God detests most.

3. In as much as it is the inner mental attitude which matters in moral affairs, morally meritorious acts cannot be enforced. As the Prophet said: "Religion is sincerity".[10]

4. As I have shown, even for apostasy the Qur'an does not demand *worldly* punishment. How, then, can other less serious actions of noncompliance be punished by people without a specific Qur'anic basis?

5. Most of the behavior forbidden in the Qur'an is not to be penalized by 'secular' punishment. It is not the business of zealous individuals to put this right.

8. 3:104, 110, 114; 7:157; 9:71, 112; 22:41; 31:17.
9. Al Nawawi, *Forty Hadith,* 3rd edition, Leicester 1977, hadith no. 34.
10. *Ibid.,* hadith no. 7.

6. The Islamic State (see the chapter "Integrism: The Islamic State") is liberal: Total enforcement of general and private morality leads inevitably to a totalitarian State.

7. It is unthinkable that God should command Muslims to protect the intellectual and moral dignity of *non-Muslims* and their freedom of conscience (2:256), and yet want to see *Muslims* subjected to compulsion.

The result of these deliberations is clear: The Qur'anic commandment to be tolerant applies among Muslims as it applies vis-à-vis non-Muslims. Everyone should ensure that what is just and right will be carried out in his environment—as a member of his family, as the boss of his factory, as the Head of State in his State—but not beyond his jurisdiction. Otherwise, as a result of misunderstood integrism, we might witness the rise of a fascist 'Islamic' State. May God protect us from this, even if such States may wish to see themselves as 'theocratic'.

REPUBLIC OR MONARCHY?

I know, I know, retrospective historical speculation is futile. Hypothetical questions such as "What would have happened if . . . ?" are just social games.

And yet it is tempting to ask oneself, what, for example, would have become of Islam if 'Ali ibn Abi Talib, obvious candidate for the Prophet's successor, had been present at the election of the first Caliph Abu Bakr, instead of devoting himself to the burial of Muhammad?

What would have happened if 'Ali, instead of 'Uthman b. 'Affan, had succeeded the second Caliph, 'Umar ibn al Khattab? Would it have been possible to connect him with the murder of 'Uthman, the actual third Caliph, which completely overshadowed 'Ali's own rule, the fourth Caliphate?

Would 'Ali' have become the involuntary founder of a 'Party' (*Shi'ah*) from which an Islamic sect—Shi'ism—would later develop?

Enough of such dizzying questions. I would like to draw two conclusions from the actual course of history in connection with this issue.

As is well known, 'Ali, like the Prophet, came from the Arab tribe of Quraysh and, like him, belonged to the Hashemite clan. As a cousin of Muhammad and—through marriage with Fāṭimah—his son-in-law as well, 'Ali was connected with Islam from his and its earliest years; historically, he is regarded as the first teenager of Islam, if not its first male convert: A man of action and of extraordinary courage, always ready to fight a duel before general battle began but at the same time a modest, pious believer, with a great deal of common sense.[1] Doubtless, 'Ali came very close to the ideal of the 'perfect man' (*al insān al kāmil*). Only very few personalities in Islamic history, amongst them 'Abd al Qadir, Algerian hero and Sufi of the nineteenth century, corresponded to the

---

1. This shines through in *Nahjul Balaghah,* a collection of 'Ali's sermons, letters, and sayings (Qum 1989), also found in Shaykh Fadhlalla Haeri; *The Sayings and Wisdom of Imam 'Ali,* Bury St. Edmunds, Suffolk, U.K., 1942.

model image of a perfect balance between body and soul to the extent 'Ali did.

There would have been these and other good reasons for choosing 'Ali as the first Caliph, including seniority and merit. But the election of a member of Muhammad's family, Āl al Bayt (People of the House), would certainly have been understood as endorsement of the monarchist principle. The other three Caliphs of the early Islamic period, on the other hand, were not direct members of the Prophet's family, although they were related to Muhammad by marriage: Abu Bakr and 'Umar—through their daughters 'Ā'ishah and Ḥafṣah—were fathers-in-law of the Prophet; 'Uthman twice became his son-in-law, through the Prophet's daughters Ruqayyah and Umm Kulthum.

The nonelection of 'Ali at the earliest stage could not prevent the monarchical idea from de facto being practiced throughout the Shi'ah world and from playing a significant role in Sunni Islam as well as for a long time. In fact, the Caliphate (until in the 16th century it was claimed by the Ottomans) remained the preserve of blood-relations of the Prophet in the widest sense (Quraysh).

Nevertheless, thanks to the process of election that preceded the appointments of Abu Bakr, 'Umar and 'Uthman, Sunni Islam retained at least a potential for universal and democratic development. The Sunni world was spared the misunderstanding that Islam is something like a religion of and for the Quraysh (or in a wider sense of and for the Arabs).

The second speculative issue concerns the question of whether, if 'Ali had been chosen as Caliph earlier, a specifically Shi'ah world, an Islamic world apart, would have grown up as it did, now comprising a belt reaching from the Lebanon to Afghanistan via Syria, Iraq, Persia, Kuwait and Bahrain.

It is probably unavoidable that a world religion which builds on previous civilizations should take on cultural traits varying from region to region. If one compares the typical Maghrib-Andalusian mosque with the Byzantine-Ottoman or Indian-Mogul mosque, this becomes quite obvious.

It was, therefore, quite normal that Islam should take on a local color in Iran, especially since in Iran it came into contact with a sophisticated culture which was famous for its richness in religious imagination, if not fantasy. (Persia after all had been home to, if not given birth to sun and fire worshippers, Zoroastrians, Mazdaeans, Nestorians, Gnostics, Neoplatonists and, later on, Assassins and Bahā'is.)

The only issue in question is whether this had to lead inevitably to the formation of an independent sect with undeniable syncretic features, as finally occurred.

What are the origins of Shi'ism, the form of Islam which commands so much attention today, despite the fact that less than 15 per cent of Muslims belong to it?[2]

It all started with a political dispute, ultimately on the matter of monarchy, which was only later given a theological basis.

We must remember that family ties and tribal connections were a matter of life and death and, therefore, almost sacred for Arab bedouins—as indeed they were throughout the entire pre-industrial world. No nomad can survive unless he belongs to a tribe, at least by adoption, either in the struggle against nature or in the fight against hostile human environment. The outlaw is as good as dead.

Imagine what it meant when, against this cult based on blood ties (today called 'national citizenship'), the Prophet set the revolutionary new principle of an ideological community, the Islamic Ummah, a brotherhood of belief—the new and best community (3:103f; 110)—that was to have priority over blood relations with non-Muslims.[3]

Those who believed and fled (from their homes) . . . and those who gave shelter and helped—these are friends and protectors of each other. (8:72)

The believers are . . . brothers. . . (49:10)

Is it still possible to appreciate what it meant when he, a distant Makkan, became head of the Madinan tribes, Pagan and Jewish, to whom he was not blood related? What it meant when the Qur'an ordered that one should abide by earlier treaties concluded with the enemy of one's friends (8:72), an absurd idea until then?

---

2. A brief overview of the Shi'ah is given by Muhammad Hossein Tabatabai, *Introduction à la Connaissance de l'Islam*, Teheran 1985; Ali Erwin Bauer, "Die Shi'iten," *CIBEDO*, Frankfurt 1990, no. 4, pp. 106–113; there is a good atmospheric description; Peter Scholl-Latour, *Allah ist mit den Standhaften*, Stuttgart, 1983, pp. 133–207.

3. Whether priority may be given amongst Muslims to blood relations is not so clear, as might be guessed from 8:75 and 33:6; see Muhammad Asad, *The Message of the Qur'an*, Gibraltar 1980, footnotes no. 86 to 8:75 and no. 9 to 33:6.

Correctly understood and practiced—as it is more extensively in the Islamic world than elsewhere—the Ummah concept means that in Islam all people are equal, regardless of their origins and the color of their skin. Only one difference counts: the extent of a person's piety. Correspondingly, the Prophet chose a black man, Bilal, as the first caller to prayer (mu'adhdhin); and he chose a Persian, Salman al Farsi, as his financial adviser. Even more importantly, he recommended no successor in order to his community to ensure that all candidates had equal opportunities.[4]

Understandably, the early Muslims assumed that those to whom Islam was first preached, whose belief had forced them to emigrate, had natural priority in the safeguarding of the Islamic heritage. This led to the Caliphate initially falling exclusively to former Makkans, i.e., members of the Quraysh, and even to a quasi-noble family such as the Banu 'Umayyah ('Uthman's clan), although it was this very family which had fought Muhammad the most vehemently.

It is this that 'Ali's supporters protested against. They did not want to make the Caliphate accessible to each and every Muslim. On the contrary, within the Quraysh they wanted to reserve it for the family of the Prophet in the narrowest sense, that is, for 'Ali and his male heirs. Even if it had not been possible to reproach 'Uthman for nepotism, this view would have brought him into sharp opposition to 'Ali.

A virtual schism (fitnah) arose when members of the Umayyah family accused 'Ali of being responsible for 'Uthman's murder in 656 because of having failed to prevent it. The outcome was the fateful (though inconclusive) battle of Siffin (657) opposing 'Ali and Mu'awiya (who in 660 proclaimed himself Caliph at Damascus while 'Ali still reigned, as fourth Caliph of Islam, in Iraq and Iran) led to:

- the first war between Muslims;
- the secession of the Kharijites sect of puritanical Muslims;[5]
- the murder of 'Ali (661) by a member of that sect, his son al Hasan's renunciation of the Caliphate, and the killing of his son al Husayn at Karbala on 10 Muharram 680.

But the most important, if not the most tragic result was that this *political* schism led gradually to the formation of an unmistakable Shi'ah reli-

---

4. 'Umar saw this; see Halid Ünal, *Al Farūq, 'Umar ibn al-Ḥaṭṭab,* Cologne 1986, p. 62.
5. The 'Ibadites in North and East Africa and in 'Uman and the Mozabites in the Algerian M'zab region are remotely related to this group.

gious identity, despite a strong intra-Shi'ah diversification.[6] (From the Shi'ah may be counted today two main stream groups: The Zaidites and the Twelvers and a number of splinter groups (like the Ismailites, Sevener Shi'ahs, Druse, Alawites,[7] Bektashis, and Ilahis).

In fact, it is not only certain aspects of Shi'ah philosophy, theology, and jurisprudence which differ from Sunni Islam, but also style and mood, in short: Atmosphere and intellectual climate. Some of these differences are:

1. According to the Shi'ah doctrine of the Caliphate—here called Imamate—only near blood-relatives of the Prophet are qualified for office.

2. The Shi'ah Imam is considered infallible both in the moral and doctrinal sense.

3. The Imam is considered as well to have insight into hidden meanings of the Qur'an.

4. 'Ali is attributed the unique title of 'Friend of God' (*wali Allah*) and in this capacity, in addition to Muhammad, he was later included into the call to prayer (*al adhān*).

5. The anniversary of the death of al Husayn is commemorated with passion plays and public mourning, including flagellation.

6. Considering the caliphate of Abu Bakr, 'Umar, and 'Uthman illegitimate Shi'ah scholars do not accept as valid prophetic traditions (*ahadith*) transmitted by them, nor those transmitted by Muhammad's wife 'A'ishah.

7. Shi'ah jurisprudence considers temporary marriages (*al mut'ah*) as legal.

A peculiar Shi'ah feature is its doctrine of the concealment (*al ghaybah*) of the so-called 'Hidden Imam'. Historical background to it is the fact that in direct Imamate line the family of Muhammad died out with the disappearance in 873-74 of the 12th Imam. Shi'iah Muslims believe that this last Imam while in 'occultation' is invisibly present, and that he will return at the end of time with the messianic function of al Mahdi, the Restorer. [8] In fact, the Iranian Constitution of 15 November 1979 in its first chapter, principle five, declares:

---

6. The sixth Shi'ah Imam, Jafar al Sadiq was regarded by the founders of the Maliki and Hanafi schools as a representative of Sunni orthodoxy, see M. M. Ahsan in *Muslim World Book Review*, Leicester 1990, no. 10, p. 13.

7. Defined by some as "Shi'ah without Shari'ah".

8. Jassim M. Husain, *The Occultation of the Twelfth Imam*, London 1982.

In the Islamic Republic of Iran the task and authority of leadership falls to the legal scholars during the absence of the concealed twelfth Imam—may God let him appear soon.

In view of this, Shi'ah religious scholars continue to administer a theocratic commonwealth, based on bloodties, in other words, a unique religious monarchy.

It is legitimate for Sunni Muslims to discuss whether the veneration shown to 'Ali is compatible with the role of Muhammad; whether Muslims should adopt a posture of structural mourning (over the death of al Husayn); whether the Caliphate should not be open to any pious Muslim; whether any human being can ever be considered infallible; whether not all the first four successors to Muhammad should be regarded as"Rightly-guided Caliphs"; whether the theory of 'hidden meanings' does not lead to an elitist or esoteric Islam; or whether certain archetypal ideas of earlier Iranian religions (Mazdaen priesthood; Manichaean black-and-white thinking) are traceable in the Shi'ah. Such questions may not lead anywhere but are legitimate.

The Sunni persecution of Shi'ah Muslims, throughout Islamic history, was, however, never legitimate. After all, there has never been any doubt that both kinds of Muslims share the same God, the same prophet, and the same book, and that they pray, fast and perform pilgrimage to Makkah in the same way.

The experience of being oppressed and persecuted for centuries has given Shi'ah psychology a particular social-revolutionary outlook. Thus the Iranian Constitution professes in its preamble to "continue this (Islamic) revolution at home *and abroad*" with the "task of preparing the way for a single community of believers *in the world*." Typically Shi'ah is principle 154 of the Constitution's 10th chapter, according to which Iran "supports the just struggle of the oppressed against the oppressor *throughout the world*." (Such sounds have not been heard in Europe since the Communist Manifesto of 1848.)

There is another consequence flowing from the Shi'ah complex of real or perceived persecution: the doctrine of *taqīyah* (dissimulation of one's belief). Certainly, all Muslims have the right to dissimulate their beliefs when it becomes a question of life and death.

Whoever expresses disbelief in God after having accepted belief
[will suffer consequences] except one who acts under compulsion
the while his heart remains true to his belief. (16:106)

Shi'ah scholars, however, seem to have extended this privilege to
Muslims who find dissimulation just more convenient or more expedient
in terms of *da'wah*.[9] (Even Ayatollah Khomeini still devoted a chapter to
this issue.)[10] Members of the Turkish Alevi sect definitely practiced this
doctrine until a few years ago when they openly entered the political
arena (on the far left).

Shi'ah scholarship has been nowhere more influential than in philosophy, a field with a rich past in Iran—just think of neo-Platonic Gnosticism
and other forms of theosophic speculation which are part of esoterism and
the Sufi heritage. Thinkers like Nasir al Din Tusi, Mir Damad, Mulla
Sadra Shirazi or Ja'far Kashfi are much to little known in the Sunni
world.[11] Indeed, most Sunnis are unaware of the fact that the doctrine of
taqlīd with its ensuing stand-still of intellectual activity was not applied
in the Shi'ah world.

Sunni Muslims, also with a view to their Shi'ah brothers, underline frequently that Islam is the 'religion of the middle way' (2:143) *par excellence,* abhorring any kind of exaggeration—from elitism and hero-wor-
ship to political revolution:[12]

And never turn your eyes in longing for whatever splendor of this
world's life We have given to so many others in order to test them.
The provision of your Lord is certainly better and more lasting.
(20:131)

But these 'democratic' features of Sunni Islam do not imply that respect
for, and veneration of, the family of the Prophet were missing in their
world. On the contrary, there are tens of thousands of Sunni Muslims
who—as *sharif* or *sayyid*—are proud to be descendants of Muhammad,
either via al Hasan or al Husayn; frequently they are popularly believed

---

9. Devin J. Steward, Taqiyyah as Performance: *The Travels of Baha al Din al 'Amili in
the Ottoman Empire (991-93 / 1583-85), Princeton Papers* vol IV, Spring 1996.

10. "Risalah fi al taqiyyah," *Al Rasa'il,* Qum 1385 h.

11. Henry Corbin, *History of Islamic Philosophy,* London 1993, devotes 43 pages to
Shi'ah thought.

12. See Martin Kraemer, *Shi'ism, Resistance and Revolution,* London 1987.

to carry a particular blessing (*barakah*). Also, as part of their ritual prayers, all Muslims every day call God's peace upon their Prophet and blessings upon him and his family (*wa 'ala Āli Muḥammad*). In addition, in many parts of the Muslim world—while not in Saudi Arabia—it has become customary since the 13th century to celebrate Muhammad's birthday in ways not too dissimilar to Christmas eve celebrations in the Christian world.[13]

It is here where Muslims of all shadings must draw the line, be it their veneration of Muhammad or of 'Ali: The line beyond which a process of deification—as in the case of Jesus—might start. When God commanded Muhammad to say: "**I am a mortal like you** (41:6)," He drew that line, and nobody should dare to cross it.

From time to time, initiatives are taken in favor of a Sunni/Shi'ah reprochement, as recently by King Hassan II of Morocco, who claims himself as a descendant of the Prophet (via al Hasan), with the aim of creating one universal Islamic school of jurisprudence (*madhhab*), including the Shi'ah school (originally based on al Imam Ja'far al Sadiq from al Madinah).[14]

I see, however, no realistic chance for a Muslim 'reunification' after 1370 lunar years of separation. Concretely, I cannot see that the Shi'ah could, or would, abandon its interpretation, out of context, of the last phrase of *Sūrat al Aḥzab* (33:33)

> ... **Because God only wishes to remove all impurities from you, oh members of the family (of Muhammad: *ahl al bayt*), and to make you pure and spotless**

as if it were an eternal divine constitutional guarantee of infallibility in doctrine and behavior. This esoteric interpretation is after all the theoretical foundation for the entire Shi'ah edifice. Nor can it be expected that both sides could agree on a common treasure chest filled with traditions of the Prophet acceptable to both sides, even if transmitted via 'Uthman or 'A'isha bint Abu Bakr.

---

13. Annemarie Schimmel has studied all forms of veneration of the Prophet, including some inacceptable one: *Und Muhammad ist Sein Prophet,* Munich 1981.

14. A private initiative for rapprochement is made by Mustafa al Rafi'i, *Islamuna,* Northwood, Middlesex 1987.

But one thing must be possible, not only because it is obligatory: That no Sunni (or Shi'ah) Muslim openly questions whether his Shi'ah (or Sunni) neighbor really is a Muslim. This is a question which according to Qur'an and Sunnah can only, and should only, be answered by God Himself.[15]

What is within reach, and what Sunni and Shi'ah Muslims can do in practical terms, may seem too little or too simple, but goes a long way: To live peacefully together and to pray with each other and for each other. That alone would be no mean feat!

---

15. *Sūrat al Nisā'* (4) *ayah* 94; *Ṣaḥīḥ Muslim,* The Book of Faith, XXVII no. 116.

INTEGRISM:
THE ISLAMIC STATE

The relations between the West and Islam have been shaped by two concepts of the State, each with different constitutional assumptions, irreconcilably opposed to each other.

On the one hand we have secularism as a global model, with its far-reaching, if not total separation of State and religion. This has been put into effect most consistently in France and Mexico, while in most other Western Republics, such as the United States, Great Britain and Germany, State and religion remain linked in some way (in religious education, school prayers, church taxes, holidays, the observance of Sunday, religious oaths). The separation of religion and State is understood as the *conditio sine qua non,* the basic pre-requisite for any true democracy based on the rule of law, political pluralism, and the separation of powers.

In opposition to this we find Islamic integrism, the concept of the integration of State and religion, even in a democratic country.

Each side has found a useful battle cry for its position. On the Christian side one likes to quote the biblical passage "Render unto Caesar that which is Caesar's and unto God that which is God's".[1] Islam responds with the slogan: *Dīn wa dawlah!* (Islam is religion and State).

Even if this formula is not found in the Qur'an, the entire Qur'anic revelation is 'integristic,' in that it sees Muslims as moral beings who should think and act in a theocentric manner at all times, i.e., in their capacity as State citizens, too. Islam takes hold of man in his entirety.

Muslims believe that Western secularism is an illusion, perhaps even self-deception, because for them it is axiomatic that:

- No State can function free of ideology: even seemingly neutral secularism is itself a *weltanschaung.* Indeed, as can be observed both in France and Turkey (Kemalism), the rejection of religion is itself a pseudo-religious ideology!; and

---

1. Perhaps Jesus was only demanding that State taxes be paid with official currency. . .

- The attempt to separate religion and the State makes people schiz-ophrenic, since no one is capable of practicing true faith on a tem-porary basis. Something has to give! A genuinely devout person cannot shed his faith as though it were clothing.

Before Macchiavelli and still well into the nineteenth century Christians held similar views. In fact, the transformation of European Christianity, into the contemporary world of secular States, was the final triumph of irreligious forces over the transcendentally anchored man. Those who had triggered this far reaching process of secularization in the 18th century—heroes of the "Age of Enlightenment" like Voltaire, King Frederic II of Prussia, Lessing and Kant—had only intended to put the domineering Churches into their place. In the end, however, they secu-larized them as well.

Since this time, the State has been mythologized and made a sacred object of worship in both West and East, based on political theories which can easily be unmasked as substitute metaphysics.[2]

For these reasons, the Islamic world reacts allergically when one of their number—the Egyptian 'Ali 'Abd al Razzaq, for example—ques-tions the principle of *dīn wa dawlah* and recommends a secular Islamic State.

The slogan quoted above does not claim that 'religion *is* the State,' but affirms that Islam is both 'religion *and* the State'. This acknowledges that the two are not identical, that we are dealing with two different entities which must be brought into a harmonious relationship with each other in an Islamic way.

Indeed, it is a much researched question whether there exists at all a definitive Islamic theory of State.[3] German orientalists such as Gustav von Grunebaum[4] and Tilman Nagel[5] tend to affirm.

This question is not easy to answer, even though there have been some (albeit very few) Islamic State theoreticians of high rank such as al Farabi

---

2. S. Parvez Manzoor, "Islam as Politics," *The Muslim World Book Review*, Leicester 1989, no. 3, pp. 3ff; Manzoor, "Politics without Truth, Metaphysics or Epistemology," *The Muslim World Book Review* 1990, no. 4, p. 3 ff.

3. A selection of the enormous volume of works includes: Alfred von Kremer, *Geschichte der herrschenden Ideen im Islam*, Leipzig 1868; Ed. K. Ferdinand und M. Mozaffari, *Islam: State and Society*, London 1988; Daniel Pipes, *In the Path of God: Islam and Political Power*, New York 1984; Bernard Lewis, *The Political Language of Islam*, Chicago 1988; P. J. Vatikiotis, *Islam and the State*, London 1987; Axel Köhler, *Islam—Leitbilder der Wirtschafts– und Gesellschaftsordnung*, Cologne 1981.

4. *Der Islam im Mittelalter*, Munich 1963.

5. *Staat und Glaubensgemeinschaft im Islam*, 2 vols, Munich 1981.

(died 950),[6] Nizam al Mulk Tusi (1018–1092)[7] and, most important of all, Abu al Hasan al Mawardi (974–1058).[8]

The problem they faced was that their work had to be developed on a minimal Qur'anic basis, thus primarily representing the 'fallible work of mortals' from the point of view of a rational fundamentalist. In fact, the Qur'an—which was revealed after the time of Plato, but before Dante, Carlyle and Hegel—does not refer to a State in the contemporary sense at all. Rather, it assumes a moral community, the Islamic 'Ummah, which guarantees the right physical and spiritual environment for the successful development of Islam.

In actual fact only three elements regarding State organization can be isolated directly from the Qur'an. (Of its more than 6,000 verses only 200 are of a normative character.) They are:

- The *presidial* principle, according to which a State president (Amir), and not a Committee or Politburo, must be head of State. He functions as a successor to the Prophet but not as a 'representative of God' in the papal sense.[9]

- The *consultative* principle, according to which executive and legislative functions must be exercised on the basis of consultation (*shūrā*)[10].

- The Islamic principle, according to which Islam is the *State religion*. This requires the head of State to be a Muslim and the entire legislation to be kept in accordance with the Qur'an Sunnah as the basic and highest constitutional law of the land, assuring of course the rights and privileges of non-Muslim minorities, too.

Indirectly, we may derive a fourth, *democratic* principle from these three. We may indeed conclude, from the rights of the 'Ummah as such (Qur'an 2:30) and the Qur'an's insistence on the administration of justice, that the obligatory consultations mentioned above should not only be advisory but *binding*. This interpretation already espoused by Muhammad 'Abdu, but also shared by Rashid Rida, the later Maulana Abu 'Ala al Maududi, Muhammad Asad, and the late Said Ramadan is today vigorously defended by Fathi Osman.[11]

---

6. See the overview in M. M. Sharif, *A History of Muslim Philosophy*, Vol. 1, Wiesbaden 1963, pp. 704ff.

7. *Traité de gouvernement (Siyasatname)*, Paris 1984.

8. See M. M. Sharif's overview, *op. cit.*, p. 717.

9. 4:59. According to 2:30 all humanbeings are 'successors' (*al Khalīfah*) on earth.

10. 3:159; 42:38.

11. Muhammad Asad, *The Message of the Qur'an*, Gibraltar 1980, footnote 122 to 3:159, and Fathi Osman, *The Children of Adam—An Islamic Perspective on Pluralism*,

On the other hand, Islamic democracy is not to be understood as unlimited sovereignty of the people, even while it is always people who have to translate God's sovereignty on earth into concrete action. Just like any other parliament, a Muslim parliament must take into account the constitution, in this case the Qur'anic norms, the shari'ah in the narrow sense of divine, i.e., Qur'anic norms. Within this broad framework an Islamic parliament is free to construct State organizations, an economic system, a system of criminal law, etc., since the Qur'an and (normative) Sunnah as well allow maximum flexibility in these matters.

Muhammad Asad has shown in his pioneering book *The Principles of State and Government in Islam* (1961), fruit of lifelong studies, that the ideal Islamic commonwealth is a State under the rule of law, a parliamentary republic with a constitution, which could correspond to Western constitutions on all essential points (separation of power, bill of rights, party pluralism, protection of minorities), as long as it ensures that the head of State is a Muslim, that Islam is the State religion, and that the Qur'an is the supreme constitutional norm.[12]

Early Islamic history laid foundations for a democratic tradition, but not in a compulsory manner: the first Caliph, Abu Bakr, was publicly chosen in 632 in the *Saqīfah* after debate, causing the withdrawal of his opponents. However, this process was not repeated, and did not become unequivocal Sunnah practice. The second Caliph, 'Umar, was chosen by acclamation in 634, i.e., without opponents. In 644 the third Caliph, 'Uthman, emerged from election by an electorate limited to six particularly well-qualified aristocrats of early Islam, including 'Ali.

Out of respect for the first believers (*al sābiqūn*), the emigrants from Makkah (*al muhājirūn*), and for the companions of the Prophet (*al ṣaḥābah*), early Muslims quite naturally demanded that both candidates and electors be specifically qualified in terms of their Islamic past. In their theories of the Caliphate (or Imamate), later generations raised their requirements of the Caliph qualification so high, at least in the Fatimid conception, that he became a "creature with a higher existential

---

Washington, D.C. 1996, pp. 46–72, are both convinced that modern parliamentary republics have Qur'anic roots. The same view is expressed by Osman, *Sharia in Contemporary Society, the Dynamics of Change in the Islamic Law,* Los Angeles 1994, pp. 74–98 (*Shura and Democracy*). Also see Fathi Osman, "Modern Islamists and Democracy," *ARABIA,* London, May 1986, p. 9; Said Ramadan, *Islamisches Recht,* Wiesbaden 1980, p. 131; Fatima Mernissi, *La Peur-modernité. Conflit Islam—democracie,* Paris 1992; *Democracy without Democrats?,* ed. Ghassan Salamé, N.Y., NY 1994.

12. Muhammad Asad, *The Principles of State and Government in Islam,* Gibraltar 1980.

quality" (Tilman Nagel). A corresponding trend in the Christian world began to go to the other extreme as the democratic era began. Finally, it became a fundamental democratic principle that nothing other than a positive election result is required as qualification for elected office. Equality before the law now means that a former lance corporal, actor, or head of the secret service must all have the same chance of reaching the highest office as a well-respected professor of political science.

In contrast, in the Islamic world personal and traditional merits and qualifications continue to be valued so highly that the climate there remains anti-populist. The figure of the 'good and just ruler' is still very much alive, especially amongst young integrists.

Against this historical background it is clear that even according to traditional interpretations, Islam allows various forms of State, including monarchies, as long as they are based on popular consensus, formal or informal, and therefore legitimate.

Having said that, it is clear that democracies are best capable of solving the core problem of every State: *quis custodiet custodes* (who controls the controllers)? Without any doubt the democratic process is proven to be the most effective one for preventing the abuse of power. It is clear that an Islamic community must cope as well with this problem of control, since the lofty ideal of applied Qur'anic values cannot come true without State institutions.

In this context, the constitution which Muhammad gave the federated city-State of Madinah, with himself as head of State (following his flight from Makkah) remains significant—at least for those who regard the early Islamic period, the 'Golden Age' of the 'Rightly guided Caliphs' (*al Khulafā' al Rāshidūn*) from 632 to 661, as a definitive model in every respect and for all times. This document, known as the *Ṣaḥīfah* or *Kitāb al Rasūl*, has been textually preserved. [13]

In my opinion there is little to be derived from this historically unique and far-sighted constitution, revolutionary as it was in terms of legal theory. Nor can anything be derived from it which might block a democratic development of Islam. The Madinah constitution, after all

- was a reaction to a very particular historical situation (with a close co-location of Jewish and Muslim tribes); and therefore,
- proved to be of an interim nature; and, most importantly,

---

13. M. Hamidullah, *The First Written Constitution in the World*, 3rd edition, Lahore 1975; Yussuf Abbas Hashmi, *Kitabu-r-Rasul—The Constitutional Dictation of Muhammad*, Karachi 1984.

- depended on the presence of not only of a charismatic but of a divinely-inspired and guided messenger, a condition which can no longer be fulfilled by any head of State.[14]

Under these circumstances it is hardly surprising that Muslims, like Christians throughout their history, can be found living in rather different types of States: shaykdoms founded on tribal loyalties; regimes based on single party systems; military dictatorships with charismatic leaders; monarchies by divine right (or grace) theocracies.[15]

Life in a true and full democracy has so far only been granted to Muslims in Malaysia and in the Diaspora.[16]

But, on the basis of what has been said above, it should also be evident that Islam by no means *demands* a nonlaical, theocratic form of State, a State analogous to Khomeini's Iran, in which power at the highest level is entrusted exclusively to theologians. On the contrary, there is not a single Qur'anic verse detailing the organization of political power in this way. In fact, in early Islam a 'clergy' did not exist. Let me repeat that *dīn wa dawlah* assumes that government and religious administration are separate functions, to be brought into harmony in the spirit of Islam, but different functions nevertheless.

But if Muslims forget that political acts are the domain of mortals; that God tolerates governments, but does not install them; that Islam knows of no clergy—then the result could be an Islamic theocracy, with the potential of degenerating into despotism, a true 'totalitarian nightmare'.[17] Theocracy in the narrow sense is, therefore, often clearly regarded as un-Islamic.[18]

---

14. But even he deferred to majority views when consultation in purely political or military matters suggested an alternative course of action, as before the Battle of Uhud (625); Muhammad had unsuccesfully argued against giving open battle.

15. Abdul Rahman Abdul Kadir Kurdi, *The Islamic State: A Study Based on the Islamic Holy Constitution,* London 1984; James V. Schall, *Reason, Revelation and the Foundation of Political Philosophy,* London 1987; Andreas Meier, *Der Politishe Austrag des Islam,* Wuppertal 1994; Abdul Rashid Moten, *Political Sciene—An Islamic Perspective,* N.Y., NY 1996.

16. Present-day Turkey cannot be regarded as an Islamic democracy, even though it does not appear to be a secular republic either. Some describe it as a country with a Muslim population but NOT a Muslim country: Abdelwahab El-Affendi, "From Istanbul with Love. . . and Fear: The Trials and Tribulations of Turkish "Secularism," *Muslim Politics Report,* N.Y., NY, no 3, May/June 1997, pp. 3, 5, 7.

17. Parvez Manzoor, *The Muslim Book Review,* 1990, no. 4, p. 12.

18. Muh. Said al Asmawy, *L'Islamisme contre l'Islam,* Paris 1989 (translation of *Al Islam al Siyasi,* Cairo 1987); Said Ramadan, *op. cit.,* p. 48.

Finally, we should clarify what concepts of the State are held by those 'integrists' who are giving Islam today a political face in Pakistan and throughout the Arab world.[19]

These 'Islamist' movements, whose founding father was the Iranian 'Pan-Islamist' Jamal al Din al Afghani (1838–1897), are critical of Western civilization, yes, but they are mainly concerned with reestablishing the dignity of their own peoples, through regaining political, cultural, and economic independence from their erstwhile colonial masters. If some of them almost involuntarily reject the Western form of democracy, too, it is because they got to know it as an instrument of colonial subjugation, attempted de-Islamization, enforced Christianization, and as a *de facto* road maker for atheism. On the other hand, most Islamist leaders, virtually all of them academics trained in Western institutions of higher learning, are highly appreciative of Western education, technology, rule of law, and the concept of human rights, as guaranteed by the Qur'an.

Believe it or not: Islam does play a great role within Islamist movements, not only for motivating and legitimizing their struggle for a change of the status quo in their home countries, Islam serves also as a vehicle for the rediscovery of identity and self-respect, a third way between capitalism and socialism, leading out of underdevelopment and into spiritual and cultural autonomy. As such Islam is a vehicle, but not only a vehicle, of a political, but not merely political, current. Since the foundation of the Egyptian Muslim Brotherhood (*al Ikhwān al Muslimūn*) and their programmatic orientation by Hasan al Banna (1906–1949)[20] the religious component has perhaps even become dominant.[21]

At any rate, it would be a great mistake, indeed, to overlook the authentic religious element within this phenomenon of renewal, without which its power and mass appeal could not be fully explained.

In the era of revolutions, it is only normal that Islamic movements, too, see in Islam a revolutionary concept, justifying violence in self-defence against systems which permit no democratic change, provoke Islam or exercise structural repression, including torture (see the chapter "Tolerance or Violence?"). It does not bother them that the concept of 'revolution' does not appear once in the Qur'an. In fact, the Qur'an assumes the necessity for *continuous* change in both the spiritual and

---

19. For an overview see *The Islamist Dilemma—The Political Role of Islamist Movements in the Contemporary Arabic World,* ed. L. Guazzone, Reading 1995.

20. *Five Tracts of Hasan al-Banna,* Chicago 1978.

21. This is definitely true for organizations like the World Assembly of Muslim Youth/WAMY in Riyadh and the Muslim Youth Movement of Malaysia/ABIM (Kuala Lumpur)

material worlds.[22] Islamist strategy corresponds to the well-known leftist revolutionary approach of 'conquering' States from the top, rather than from below, which requires more patience. This issue implies more than mere tactics. It is an issue that has split the intellects within contemporary Islamic revival movements. Those, like the Pakistani al Tabligh al Islami, who start from the assumption that an Islamic State can only be brought about through the formation of truly Islamic personalities, concentrate on 'grass roots work,' focusing on the individual and intra-Islamic missionary work. Others, including some in England and Germany, founded Islamic political parties on the spot, or try to form cadres near centers of power, like the Spanish Catholic lay organization, *Opus Dei*.

Despite my personal contact with several leaders of integrist or Islamist groups, I am not in a position to predict what kind of States would emerge from their political victory be it in Algeria or Tunisia, Jordan or Egypt, even though more and more of their leaders, like Rashid Ghannushi, exiled *amir* of the Tunesian MTI (*Mouvement de la Tendance Islamique*) and the leadership of the Egyptian *Ikhwan al Muslimun,* come out for democracy (including a multiparty system and women's rights to elected office).[23]

Analytically, it is hard to know where to start with agenda items such as "The Qur'an is our constitution" (Hasan al Banna) and theses such as "There are only two parties: the Party of God and the Party of Satan" or "all sovereignty lies with Allah" (*al ḥākimīyah li Allah*) as long as the concrete understanding of 'shari'ah' remains vague. Unfortunately, I have reason to suspect that when they speak of 'introducing the shari'ah' even leading representatives of Islamic reform movements do not mean a shari'ah limited to divine law, but the entire edifice of Islamic jurisprudential orthodoxy as developed by the 14/15th century.[24]

Wherever and whenever this is the case, radical Muslims (integrists, Islamists) meet with conservative Muslims (traditionalists, orthodox Muslims) in a community of action.

But this phenomenon—the meeting of extremes—is hardly new.

22. Hamam Boukhari, "Le Coran et la Révolution," *El-Moujahid,* Algiers, 27. 4. 1989, p. 13.

23. See Abdelbaki Hermassi, "The Rise and Fall of the Islamic Mouvement in Tunisia," in *The Islamist Dilemma,* op. cit., pp. 105–129; Rashid Ghanoushi, *Al Hurriyāt al 'Ammah fi al Dawlah al Islamīyah,* Beirut 1993; "Statement of the Muslim Brotherhood on the Role of Muslim Women in Islamic Society on Human Rights, and on the Multi-Party System in an Islamic Society," *Encounters* vol 1, no 2, (Leicester) 1995, pp. 85–103.

24. How justifiable this suspicion is may be seen in Roswitha Badry, "Mustafa Kamal Wasfi und der Traum von einer 'islamischen Verfassung,'" in *Gottes ist der Orient— Gottes ist der Okzident, Festschrift für A. Falaturi,* 1991, p. 83 ff.

ISLAMIC MARKET ECONOMY

In so far as Islam provides instruction on the right way to behave in all spheres of life, it also provides instructions for dealing with the productive forces—work, landed property, and capital—in short, for the right way to organize economic life.

But in this sphere too, as in the Islamic State theory (see the previous chapter), the Qur'an contains very few and only basic principles. For very good reasons, as it turns out, Qur'an and Sunnah have a great deal to say on how Muslims should behave as producers, consumers, and holders of capital, but little on their economic *system*. Islam is geared toward the moral aspects of the economic sphere, which is true for its attitude towards the social system in general. It is primarily concerned with economic *ethics*.

Nevertheless, there are some important Qur'anic framework conditions that every economic order calling itself Islamic must reflect.

1. The Qur'an calls for *private ownership* as a matter of principle, also as far as the means of production are concerned. In legal theory individual ownership must, however, not be construed to resemble absolute property in Roman law; rather, since the whole of Creation belongs to God alone, as usufruct with strong social strings attached to it.[1] This qualified form of 'ownership' takes precedence over the exceptional possible ownership of the State and of private foundations.[2] Natural resources such as air, water, woods, pasture land, and mineral resources cannot be privately owned; however, the government may issue licenses for their use.[3]

2. Muslims are obliged to earn their livelihood through honest, productive *work* and not through begging, speculation or bribes, even

---

1. The alternative concept of 'dual property' (held by God and man) is erroneous; see Akhtar A. Awan, *Quality, Efficiency and Property Ownership in the Islamic Economic System*, Boston 1983.

2. It is important to emphasise this in view of the enormous abuse of State and private foundation property throughout history. In the eighteenth century 2/3 to 3/4 of the Ottomans' land property was owned by foundations; family foundations contributed to the financial ruin of the Ottoman Empire; see J. R. Barnes, *An Introduction to Religious Foundations in the Ottoman Empire*, Leiden 1986.

3. As one might imagine, this possibility is challenged in view of the role played by Western oil companies in Muslim countries.

if they are called 'commissions'. This includes trade for profit within a market which allows the free formation of prices, e.g., by prohibiting monopolies. (In Makkah, Muhammad was a paid employee in the import–export firm owned by his wife, Khadijah.) Speculative profit, not gained by any real effort or without risk (e.g., on the stock exchange, futures market, or as interest on capital) is prohibited. (We must return to this subject.)

3. The State must supervise the *market* (in order to prevent monopolies, false weights, and other forms of economic crime).

4. Through legislation, particularly in the area of customs and taxation, Muslim governments should promote *social justice*. This aim is also served by Qur'anic provisions for inheritance and taxation (although the scale of the tax [zakah] is not progressive), and by the prohibition of hoarding and of luxury. The leveling of wealth or income is, however, not the sociopolitical ideal of Islam.

5. Muslims should be neither misers nor spendthrifts. As in all things they are encouraged to be moderate also as a consumer, though not to become an ascetic.

Beyond this framework the Qur'an guarantees every flexibility for the concrete organization of an economic system, a fact that reflects divine wisdom. Economic challenges change so continually that the history of economic thought (from the school of Adam Smith to those of David Ricardo, Thomas Malthus, Karl Marx, John Maynard Keynes and Paul A. Samuelson) reads like a history of economic errors, even though each theory seemed to be correct in its time.

Contemporary Islamic economic science has made great efforts to devise a specifically Islamic economic system, though with little practical success.[4]

---

4. As the quarterly *Index of Islamic Literature* of the Islamic Foundation in Markfield (Leicester) shows, the literature on Islamic economy is so voluminous that it can hardly be mastered any more. For an introduction in German see Volker Nienhaus, *Islam und moderne Wirtschaft—Positionen, Probleme und Perspektiven*, Graz 1982, or A. Ghanie Ghaussy, *Das Wirtschaftsdenken im Islam*, Berne 1989; For English literature see the "Review of Islamic Economics," *Journal of the International Association for Islamic Economics*, published since 1992 in Arabic and English by the Islamic Foundation at Markfield, Leicester, U.K.; M. A. Mannan, *Islamic Economics: Theory and Practice*, London 1986 and his *Abstracts of Researches in Islamic Economics*, Jeddah 1984; M. Umer Chapra, *Islam and Economic Development*, Islamabad 1993; Syed Nawab Haider Naqvi, *Ethics and Economics—An Islamic Synthesis*, Leicester 1981.

Such a system is advanced as an alternative, both to Western capitalism, which idolizes the ostensibly autonomous individual, and to the planned economy of former Eastern socialism, which through its infatuation with what is 'collective' idolizes the State. Following Max Weber and Müller-Armack[5] it is possible to see *both* materialistic systems not as unreligious, but as ideologies based on perverted religious values. Islam may be held up to both systems as the only ideology which brings the individual and the State into a balanced relationship, a system which already 1400 years ago, in Madinah, produced a degree of social and economic justice of which Marx could only dream.[6]

On the other hand, a certain romantic blurring of reality is typical of this Islamic theorizing. Not all of those who have mastered the Qur'an have also mastered economics. The economy, too, follows its own laws. Profitability, for example, cannot be commanded. And the injunction that morals and economics should form an Islamic synthesis (Syed Naqvi) does not assure that they do. As the bankrupt Communist system illustrated, one cannot perform magic with economic data. It should be clear to all Muslim economists that an Islamic economic system, in the ideal sense, must be preceded by an Islamic 'Ummah, in the ideal sense.

Alas, it is also clear that some Muslim authors hold on to what may be described as collectivistic ideas and, therefore, portray the Islamic State as a welfare State[7]—which is hardly surprising when such authors come from a Marxist background.[8] From an objective analysis of the true Qur'anic framework for the economy, it is more correct to conclude that an Islamic economy should correspond, in essence, to the Western social market economy as realized in Germany, Great Britain, Switzerland, and the Netherlands.

But this of course without copying its excesses, such as the tolerance, even financial exploitation, of trade with toxic products such as alcohol, tobacco, and the so-called soft drugs. Nor should Muslims copy the degeneration of financial markets in economies pursuing 'growth' at any social cost—encouraged by the anonymity of stock companies under corporate law.

Finally, an Islamic economy might differ in that companies with limited responsibility would perhaps not exist, and in that interest on internal

---

5. See Müller-Armack, *Religion und Wirtschaft*, 2nd edition, Berne 1968.

6. Ziauddin Ahmed, "Concept and Models of Islamic Banking: An Assessment," in *The Muslim World*, 7, 14 and 28 September, 1985.

7. Z. Ahmed, *op. cit.*, 14. 9. 1985, p. 2.

8. Roger Garaudy, *L'Islam vivant*, Algiers 1986, p. 93, accepts profit only in order to measure efficiency.

and external loans would be prohibited. Both are linked, perhaps even inextricably.

Islamic law does not easily accept the concept of fictitious persons created by decree, contract, or testament, i.e., legal subjects who are virtual but not living people. Although this principle cannot be found directly in Qur'an or Sunnah, still it is the firm result of a development in Islamic jurisprudence which might well have gone in the other direction. Indeed, Muslim States today do regard themselves as legal persons under administrative, private and international law. Even beyond this, they provide a legal basis for foundations (awqāf), thus perpetuating the will of the testator beyond his death—a legal fiction closely resembling a Western 'legal person'. This should help to ease the development of a modern Islamic capital market.

Interest payment is another matter altogether. It is not only disapproved of in the Qur'an (as in 30:39 and 3:130), but is actually prohibited, albeit without explanation by the Prophet, in the final revelation, the ayat al ribā (2:275 f.), which was revealed only a few weeks before his death:

Those who devour usury behave like he whom Satan has confounded by his touch. Because they say, "Trading is like usury." But God has permitted trade and forbidden usury. . .

Elimination of ribā is not like the elimination of murder because interest has a socio-political function (which murder does not). Every first-year student at the London School of Economics or at the Harvard Business School knows how important an economic tool interest is for the accumulation of capital, profitability control, wealth creation, resource allocation, and economic policy—influencing business cycles through the stimulation of growth and the control of inflation. It is for this reason that, despite Jewish,[9] Christian and Islamic prohibitions, the world has never been entirely free from capital interest. Even today Arab oil States, even including Pakistan,[10] prefer to invest their wealth in the West at favorable rates of interest. In common with other Muslim States, the Kingdom of Morocco issues itself high interest loans.

In view of the many roles interest plays in a world which is, after all, not altruistic but greedy, Muslim lawyers have never stopped trying to

---

9. Deut. 23:20 ff.: only prohibits on collecting interest from fellow Jews.

10. In vain, every one of Pakistan's Constitutions (1956, 1962, 1973) called for the abolishment of interest (ribā).

reduce the impact of the Qur'anic prohibition of interest, or to make it seem compatible with the existing capital system. Examples are 'mark-up sales' between a bank and its client that dress up a loan as a purchase.

In Makkah it had been normal practice to charge 50 percent interest, even on a consumer credit, which guarded against starvation if a harvest failed. If repayment was delayed this charge doubled to 100 per cent. Given these circumstances, it is not entirely unreasonable to ask whether *ribā,* in the sense of verse 2:275, does perhaps not refer to 'interest,' but to 'exorbitant rates of interest' ('usury' in today's sense of the word)— perhaps even only to consumer credit.[11] But this interpretation contradicts the fact that trade credit was known in Makkah at that time and that verse 2:275 does not speak of "the doubling and redoubling of interest," even though the Qur'an uses this terminology in other places (e.g., 3:130).

Today, some people are trying to justify the taking of what amounts to interest in consideration of opportunity costs (lost profit). This is an attempt to portray interest as a price—not for the loan as such but—for the lost opportunity of gaining profit incurred by the donor as a result of having given his capital as a loan. I consider this a flagrant attempt at avoiding a clear injunction. The situation is different, however, in cases of rampant inflation. In such a cases, indexation should be allowed, otherwise account holders would be forced to make huge voluntary gifts to their banks.

However, mainstream Islamic teaching maintains the unqualified Qur'an prohibition of interest, against all odds, allowing profit from capital only when it results from a share in the enterprise of the credit-taker or by other methods of profit and risk sharing.[12] For example, if all or individual moneylenders share in the management (*mushārakah*), although they may also leave management to others (*muḍārabah*), acting as passive or 'sleeping,' though still liable, partners. In both cases, the decisive factor is that the moneylender *shares not only profits but also any losses made.* This, then, is the decisive principle of an interest-free system of money trade and banking. It seems to me that this could be a

---

11. For this reason some would allow a certain low amount of interest to be charged, up to what is needed to off-set inflation. These include A. Yusuf Ali, *The Holy Qur'an,* Brentwood 1983, footnote 324 to 2: 275; Muhammad Asad, *The Message of the Qur'an,* Gibraltar 1980, footnote 35 to 30:39; A. G. Ghaussy, *op. cit.,* p. 61–68.

12. Major Muslim economic experts like Umer Chapra and Khurshid Ahmad maintain that any kind of predetermined return on capital is forbidden. See Ahmad et al., *Elimination of Riba from the Economy,* Islamabad 1994; Chapra, *Towards a Just Monetary System,* Leicester 1985, and *Islam and the Economic Challenge,* Herndon, VA, 1992.

major Islamic contribution to the revitalization of the Western economy: Insisting on the entrepreneurial spirit of capitalism and reenforcing it.

Whether an interest-free economy will succeed has yet to be seen. Given that resources are scarce, even an interest-free capital market must prove to be in a position to:

• concentrate capital, and to

• direct it into profitable projects.

Those who must achieve this task without the mechanism of interest face a problem on which the socialist planned economy floundered (albeit for other reasons as well).

So Muslims have good reasons to gaze spellbound in the direction of Kuala Lumpur, Islamabad, Riyad, Khartoum and Teheran. Surely one of these countries should succeed in creating an efficient Islamic economy, an economy with a moral face, an economy for the people!

ISLAM AND THE ENVIRONMENT

No Muslim would dare to suggest that contemporary environmental problems were first discerned in the Islamic world. There is no doubt that this merit goes to the Club of Rome, whose 1972 report on 'The Limits of Growth' hit the occidental world like a bombshell. As one of its members, I still clearly remember how the Policy Planning Staff at the German Foreign Office was entrusted with an analysis of the consequences of the report's pessimistic findings for foreign policy.

It would be just as cheeky to maintain that until now Islamic countries had been particularly concerned about their ecology. On the contrary, German Foreign Minister Hans-Dietrich Genscher's Statement on 25 September 1991 at the General Assembly of the United Nations in New York applies to them too: "Man is still waging war against Creation!" But, since many Islamic States are part of the underdeveloped Third World, the Western countries' expensive projects for the protection, on a global scale, of the environment seems to them a luxury which only a highly industrialized First World can afford. Others, like James P. Pinkerton, see the current preoccupation with ecology merely resurgent romanticism, 'Environmanticism'.[5]

There is more than a grain of truth in this, and it is particularly inappropriate for Europeans to behave with the moral zeal of environmental missionaries. Neocolonialism could indeed enter through the (ecological) back door.

Like Germany as a whole so German Muslims, too, especially Ahmad von Denffer,[1] Harun Behr[2] and Axel Köhler[3] have been concerned with laying the foundations of environmental ethics ever since the first shock over environmental destruction. "The Environmental Question and Islam" became the main theme of the 25th anniversary of the Islamic center in Aachen on 17 May 1989.

---

1. Ahmad von Denffer, "Koran und Umwelt," *Al Islam,* Munich 1983, no. 5/6, pp. 2 ff.; "Die Umweltfrage und der Islam," *Al Islam* 1989, no. 2, pp. 20 ff.

2. Harun Behr, "Zurück-zur-Natur-Religion," *Al Islam* 1985, pp. 5 ff.

3. Axel Köhler, "Islamische Umweltethik—Versuch einer normativen Standortbestimmung," in *Gottes ist der Orient—Gottes ist der Okzident, Festschrift für A. Falaturi,* Cologne 1991, pp. 54 ff.

The essential points of an Islamic earth-first politics may be summarized as follows:[4]

1. The true cause of the catastrophic environmental destruction is the
   hubris of modern man who has become godless, who believes himself to be the unlimited master of his environment and who unleash-
   es his boundless hedonistic consumer passion on nature as if it had
   no right of its own to exist intact. The Muslim, on the other hand,
   knows that nothing belongs to him since everything belongs to God,
   that he does not inhabit the earth in order to gain mastery over it in
   the biblical sense, but in order to use it responsibly in the sense of
   usufruct.[6]

2. God expects Muslims to show moderation in all matters and not to
   waste resources under any circumstances:

   Verily, He does not love the wasteful. (6:141)

   In particular this is expressed in the requirement to avoid all pomp
   and luxury, and in the principle of never to continue eating when
   one is full.
   Generally speaking, this boils down to the principle of maintaining
   the ecological equilibrium, as expressed in the Qur'anic maxim:

   **So do not spread corruption on earth after it has been so well
   ordered. (7:56)**

   In his respect for the well designed order of nature the Muslim is,
   therefore, its born protector, even if no catastrophe looms.[7]

3. The Qur'an is almost bursting with descriptions of nature, whose
   aim it is to instill in man a sense of respect for God's creation (seen
   as the best proof possible of God's existence). For the Muslim, the
   entire Cosmos is a community united in the adoration and glorification of God.

---

4. For an alternative concise restatement of Qur'anic ecology see Iris Safwat, *Islam and
Environmental Protection*, Islam Today (ISESCO), Rabat 1994, no. 11, pp. 79–89.

5. *Environmanticism—The Poetry of Nature as Political Force*, Foreign Affairs,
May/June 1997.

6. Qur'an 6:165

7. Muslims are not prone to dooms-day thinking even while they are ready any day for
the 'day'. It would therefore be wrong to suspect them of considering the environmental
predicament as imminent 'eco-dämmerung' (Pinkerton), after Richard Wagner's
Götterdämmerung (Twilight of the Gods—End of the World).

Externally, this is expressed in the fact that numerous surahs are named after animals or natural phenomena.[8] In this context it is important that man, himself a creature and therefore part of nature, is in certain respects placed on the same level as the rest of the animate world. This is expressed in the following poetic formulation from the Qur'an:

There is no animal walking on earth nor any bird flying on its two wings which is not a creature like you. (6:38)

Let us be clear about this: for the Muslim wild animals are not ownerless animate objects in the sense of the Civil Law, but—like domesticated animals as well—members of an Ummah (of cats, dogs, horses, etc.), just as the Muslim himself is a member of the Islamic Ummah! In this spirit the Prophet Muhammad often intervened lovingly on behalf of tortured or needy animals, even little birds.[9]

This does not exclude that man is also a beneficiary of the animal world, but only within the bounds of what is permissible—killing merely animals for sport or causing them anguish is prohibited.

4. The Qur'an is neither an oracle nor an encyclopedia of the natural sciences. Nonetheless, it contains alarming descriptions of things which are currently taking place in the environment. An example of this, pointed out by A. von Denffer, is the phenomenon of acid rain mentioned in *Surat al Wāqi'ah* 56, verse 68–70:

Did you ever observe the water you drink? Do you send it down from the clouds, or do We? If we wanted We could certainly make it saltish and bitter; why then are you not thankful?

5. Of similarly fundamental significance, also for ecology, is the Prophet's famous statement that "cleanliness is half of faith." Does not the destruction of the environment often begin with its pollution?[10]

---

8. These include the cow, the cattle, the thunder, the bee, the light, the ants, the spider, the mountain, the star, the moon, the signs of the zodiac, the night star, the dawn, the sun, the night, the morning, the fig tree, the elephant.

9. For Hadith references see A. von Denffer, *op. cit.,* p. 24f. and 27.

10. Al Nawawi, *40 Hadith,* Hadith no. 23, handed down by Muslim; *Sahīh Muslim, hadith no. 432.*

Those who heed all this will not find the solution to our environmental problems, like Holger Schleip, in a new 'back to nature' religion, and certainly not in a fashionable 'green' romanticism of nature. Idolizing nature cannot reverse the environmental consequences of denying God.

Ferdinand Fellmann, who warned against the sentimental fantasies of a new philosophy of nature, was right when he established that "the true philosophical desideratum, which emerges from the threatened environmental catastrophes, is not a new philosophy of nature, but rather a new philosophy of technology".[11] What is needed is not a sentimental neopantheism, but recovery of the lost rationality of a hypertrophic, autonomous technology. In short, we need a new approach to pursuing our economic necessities.

Many of the young people in 'green' circles have realized this and have even been accused of endulging in 'greenolatry'. They have noticed that the anthropocentric view of the world cannot be reversed by voluntary self-limitation. In fact, nature can be saved by nothing less than a revolutionary change of Western man's attitude as a consumer. Only when he sees himself, as the Muslim does, as 'abd (servant of God), can such a revolution take place.

And so, many 'green' people have found their way to Islam after having followed a false alternative. Some of them had indulged (almost lustfully) in their anxiety over the existential (and thus unavoidable) risks of life. Initially, their fears were a mere symptom of the value crisis in Western society. Then these same fears became the decisive impulse for seeking and finding peace in submission to God. That is Islam.

---

11. *Frankfuter Allgemeine Zeitung*, 18 February, 1987.

ART AND THE
PROHIBITION OF IMAGES

In contrast to the Byzantine, Lutheran, and Calvinist world, the Islamic world did not experience iconoclastic riots. But it too developed a theology of figurative representation that bans iconolatry at any level. This is based not on the Qur'an, but on traditions of the Prophet[1] whose distant background is the Qur'anic assertion that God will forgive everything except idolatry (4:48).

According to the Sunnah, the production and use of pictures and statues is undesirable if they portray living creatures, in as much as this might lead to modern forms of idolatry.[2]

In this respect, Muslims are once bitten, twice shy; for pre-Islamic Arabs had not only portrayed their goddesses al Lat, al 'Uzza and Manat in stone but had also displayed these and other statues inside the Ka'bah. The Prophet was particularly outraged at the figures of Abraham, Ishmael and Mary found there.

The rationale behind this prohibition—to prevent even the slightest risk of magic and idolatry—shines through in its exceptions; for example, children's toys are allowed. ('Āyishah was still playing with dolls as the very young bride of the Prophet.) So are passport photographs, anatomical representations, and unreal, relatively abstract images, particularly if they appear on objects that may be sat or walked upon, for example, cushions or carpets. However, images of God, the prophets, and any figurative decoration of mosques are absolutely forbidden. The latter is remarkable because very old mosques, such as those in Madinah, *al Quds* (Jerusalem), and Damascus are richly decorated with floral designs or landscapes.[3]

In the past, Islamic countries were less inhibited. We need only consider Persian miniature art which emerged from 1200 onwards, or the por-

---

1. See *Ṣaḥīḥ al Bukhari*, Book 54, Hadith nos. 449 f., 539, 570 f.; Imam Malik, *al Muwaṭṭa*, Ch. 54.3, Hadith nos. 6–8.
2. See Ahmad von Denffer, *Kleines Wörterbuch des Islam*, Lützelbach 1986, p. 31; Muh. Hamidullah, *Introduction to Islam*, 5th edition, Luton 1980, para 482.
3. See Roger Garaudy, *Mosquée—Miroir de l'Islam*, Paris 1985.

trait gallery of Ottoman Sultans. The painting of miniatures was justified quite well by the argument that they only used highly stylized stock figures. In contrast, the justification of portrait painting given by Great Mogul Akbar (1556–1605) smacks of sophistry. He refused to accept that a portrait was an 'image' unless it reproduced every single hair of the subject.

Today hardly any ruler in the Muslim world outside of Saudi Arabia shies away from having himself displayed on stamps, in public places and in shops—as a mark of honor, i.e., the very motive which Islamic teaching distrusts most strongly.

By and large the prohibition of figurative representation in Islam has not been detrimental. Rather, it promoted the flourishing of arabesque design, particularly in mosaics and engravings, of calligraphy and book ornamentation. Qur'anic calligraphy became a determining feature of Islamic architecture.

This brings us to a more interesting subject: What is the Islamic view of art as such?

Like every religion with its sights set on the Afterlife, Islam does not encourage the development of 'art for art's sake'. A Muslim is not allowed to waste time.[4] He lives in a world which is portrayed to him as a mere 'sport and brief pleasure' compared to the better residence in the Afterlife (6:32). Art must appear to be frivolous to a Muslim tending towards the ascetic.

> **Are you more satisfied with this worldly life than with the life to come? But compared with the hereafter the enjoyment of life in this world is paltry. (9: 38)**

To this is added a specific reservation against poetry (26:224–226), especially in view of the slander suffered by Muhammad at the hands of satirical poets who insinuated that he had invented the Qur'an. That music and dance was suspected of being connected with sexual license and prostitution, shows realism. In Europe, too, until the 19th century, theater people had a notoriously bad reputation.

But the Islamic world—always intent on maintaining the happy medium—has never forgotten that the Qur'an calls for the enjoyment of the beautiful and good things of this world, including food and drink.

---

4. *Ṣaḥīḥ Muslim*, Ch. 940, Hadith 5551f.

Say: "Who is there to prohibit the beauty which God has produced for His servants and (His) wholesome provisions?" Say: "These are for those who believe in the life of this world—to be theirs alone on Resurrection Day." (7: 32)

Against this background the Muslims pray daily:

Our Lord! Grant us what is good in this world and what is good in the hereafter. (2:201)

An even clearer platform for the development of an Islamic ethic of the aesthetic stems from the conviction that God, as the absolutely Perfect One (al Kāmil) must also be the Beautiful One,[5] He who, according to an oft-cited Hadith, loves beauty (inna Allah jamīlun, yuḥibbu al-jamāl).[6]

And what beauty Islamic art has produced! Particularly in the fields of literature, the art of book-making, calligraphy, miniatures, architecture and the recitation of the Qur'an.

Since the first great exhibition of Islamic art in the West took place in 1912 in Vienna, European art historians have, with scientific precision, recorded, measured, weighed, drawn, reproduced and described everything that is regarded a priori as Islamic art and analyzed what is actually Islamic about it.[7]

The problem with defining Islamic art is not due to the fact that, from the beginning, Islamic art was open to foreign artists and influences (to which the great Mosque of Damascus bears witness, as do the Süleymaniye in Istanbul and the modern pilgrims' terminal at Jeddah airport). Rather the problem is rooted in the fact that Islamic art has not

---

5. However, "the Beautiful One" is not one of the names of God found in the Qur'an and is not contained in any traditional list of His '99 most beautiful names'; see Daniel Gimaret, Les noms divins en Islam, Paris 1988, pp. 215f.

6. Ṣaḥīḥ Muslim, Kitab al Iman, bāb tahrīm al kibr wa bayanihi, hadith 147; Al Tirmidhi, hadith 1999. Also see Mishkat al Masabīḥ, hadith 725.

7. For a selection in German, I recommend Ernst Kühnel, Die Kunst des Islam, Stuttgart 1962; Katharina Otto-Dorn, Kunst des Islam, 2nd edition, Baden-Baden 1966; Alfred Renz, Geschichte und Stätten des Islam, Munich 1977; Heinz Jürgen Sauermost/W. Christian von der Mühle, Istanbuler Moscheen, Munich 1981; John Hoag, Islamische Architektur, Stuttgart 1976; in English: Michael Barry, Colour and Symbolism in Islamic Architecture, London 1996; The Turkish Contribution to Islamic Arts, Yapı ve Kredi Bankasi, Istanbul 1976; Muhittin Serin, Türk Hat Üstadları, 2 vol., Istanbul 1992; Nurhan Atasoy, Splendors of the Ottoman Sultans, Memphis, Tennessee, 1992.

emerged from a specific people or a specific region, but from a specific religious point of view—and it is this which makes it so unique.

As a resigned Oleg Grabar had suggested, as the result of his pioneering studies, a work of art should be described as Islamic if it "bears or could bear Arabic script." However, many are not satisfied with such positivism. John Hoag, too, appears to start from a tautology that Islamic art is—art made by Muslims.[8] But Richard Ettinghausen's attempt at definition is just as impractical, even while he focuses on characteristics of quality: "The overall harmony, the balance of individual parts and the perfect composition" seem to him to be "always present and, therefore, the most significant Islamic element".[9] Of course, the same could be said of every classical masterpiece in any other style.

And yet, even a child can see that Islamic art has produced an unmistakable canon of form,[10] which has had a lasting influence on the Western world, particularly between the tenth and the fourteenth century.[11]

Islamic art, this much is certain, translates into form and substance a religious feeling and way of life, Islamic moral feelings as much as religious dogma. In Islamic architecture, for example, we find the ideal of 'being rather than appearing' realized, not only in houses, but in palaces too.[12] Both screen off their interior, just as Muslim women hide their 'treasures' with the 'abāyah (the long robe). Equally symbolic is the anti-hierarchical spatial arrangement of mosques and their brightness, banishing magic, the high degree of ornamental abstraction protecting our imagination against artistic manipulation; the human proportions of buildings; the arrangement and equipment of gardens, conjuring up paradise with their shady green and the cozy splashing of their fountains.

Can these phenomena not be understood and defined?

The question of definition is not just academic; the answers given betray whether art historians have an antenna for the many-layered spiritual background to Islamic art. It is to the credit of those already men-

---

8. John D. Hoag, *op. cit.*

9. Richard Ettinghausen, "Die angewandten Künste und die Malerei: Merkmale und Wirkungsbereich," in *Das Vermächtnis des Islam,* Vol. 2, Munich 1983, p. 53.

10. See Klaus Brisch, *Catalogue, Museum für Islamische Kunst,* Berlin, 2nd edition, 1980, p. 9.

11. See catalogue of the exhibition "Europa und der Orient 800–1900," in Berlin (28. 5—27. 8. 1989), *Gütersloh* 1989; Richard Ettinghausen, "Der Einfluß der angewandten Künste und der Malerei des Islams auf die Künste Europas," in *Das Vermächtnis des Islams,* Vol. 2, Munich 1983.

12. The modesty of palaces of the Royal family in 'Amman (Hashemite Kingdom of Jordan) is exemplary.

tioned that they have discovered why Islamic art is such a coherent world: because religion has a dominant influence on it. The orientalist Rudi Paret has made a major contribution to this truism with his book on *Symbolism in Islam* (1958).

Since then writing the history of Islamic art, within the Islamic world too,[13] has concentrated increasingly on questions of meaning. The highest level of awareness in art is now regarded as the metaphysical or mystical—as maintained by the Sorbonne Professor Alexandre Papadopoulo (*L'Islam et l'art islamique*), and the late Swiss Muslim Titus Burckhardt (*Die Kunst des Islam*). Let us hope that the times have passed when, for example, ignorance of the Light Verse (24:35) led some to see the empty prayer niche (*miḥrab*)of the mosque as a symbol for the absent statue of God.

Even the mathematics of Islamic ornamentation has now been researched. Thus, we now know that there exist only 17 symmetrical arrangements which allow endless expansion.[14] In this search for hidden structural elements the following seem to me to be the most important verifiable insights.

There seems to be a connection between the Arab aesthetic principle of repetition (in the Qur'an, Arab literature and music, and in *dhikr* prayer), triggering a state of ecstasy, on the one hand, and the attempts to portray God's infinity on the other—and that *both* aspects are present in arabesques and other unending ornamentation.[15]

A similar relationship has been suggested between the phenomenon of completely filling surfaces with mosaics, stucco, and carved or painted ornamentation, appearing to the uninitiated as a *horror vacui* (fear of empty spaces), and the attempt to comprehend the omnipresence of God.

Such efforts are not an attempt to 'portray' God symbolically, but to approach the essence of His being. J. C. Bürgel has reduced this approach very well to its common denominator in his article "Ekstase und Ordnung" (Ecstasy and Order).[16] His theory is that in unending, space-

---

13. See Roger Garaudy, *op. cit.*; Titus Burckhardt, *The Art of Islam,* London 1976, and *Fez, City of Islam* (1960), Cambridge, U.K. 1992; Nader Ardalan, *The Sense of Unity, The Sufi Tradition in Persian Architecture,* Chicago 1973. Of course excesses sometimes occur: Umar R. Ehrenfels, *Weibliche Elemente in der Symbolik des Islam, Zeitschrift für Missionswissenschaft und Religionswissenschaft* 1975, pp. 44ff.

14. An ornament with the highest possible number of symmetries was found in a *madrasah* in Fes; see *Süddeutsche Zeitung,* 15. 6. 1987, p. 12.

15. See Lois Lamya al Faruqi, "Die islamische Kunst," in *Weltmacht Islam,* Munich 1988.

16. *Neue Zürcher Zeitung,* 5. 4. 1991, p. 39.

filling Islamic decorations two seemingly opposing categories are united: divine order and regularity (*niẓām*) on the one hand, and the endless repetition of motifs which symbolizes (and brings about) ecstasy on the other.

As the English say: there is more to it than meets the eye.

ISLAMIC JURISPRUDENCE

Just as connoisseurs agree that there are three great cuisines, the Chinese, the French, and the Turkish, legal experts should not find it hard to agree on the three most important legal systems: the edifices of Roman, Anglo-Saxon and Islamic law, with their places of pilgrimage at Bologna, Oxford, Harvard, and Cairo. Cairo is the burial place of Imam Muhammad b. Idris al Shāfi'i (767–820), the most talented Muslim jurist of all time. His *Risālah,* a treatise on the foundation of Islamic jurisprudence,[1] and the equally fundamental Qur'an commentary *(tafsir)* of al Tabari (839–923) are ranked in intellectual history as highly as the compilation of the *Corpus Juris Civilis* of Justinian (circa 534).

Originally, these three great legal systems were similar, in so far as they owe their development to jurisprudence rather than legislation. There was university-made law in the Roman and Islamic legal systems and judge-made law in the case of Common law.[2]

Nevertheless Islamic and European law—with the exception of Canon Law—differed from the outset in that only Islamic law regarded itself as a revealed law in the narrowest sense, that is, as a genuinely divine law. It is therefore described as the clearly mapped out 'path' to salvation *(shari'ah),* which must be followed, or as specifically Islamic jurisprudence *(fiqh),* literally, understanding/insight/knowledge.

None of this has changed. However, since the beginning of the 20th century, attempts has been made to sharpen the definition of the terms *shari'ah* and *fiqh* in order to separate the core of the revealed law from lawyers' law based upon and derived from it but, nevertheless, man-made.[3]

Islamic law is essentially different from Western law with regard to its legal sources, and also with regard to its litigable area: in Islam there is

---

1. Al Shafi'i, *Risala,* 2nd edition, Cambridge 1987; Al Tabari, *The Commentary on the Qur'an,* Vol. 1, Oxford 1987.

2. Codification has become more significant now, not only in the Islamic but also in the Anglo-Saxon legal world .

3. Muhammad Asad, *This Law of Ours,* Gibraltar 1987, pp. 1–66; Asad, *The Principles of State and Government in Islam,* Gibraltar 1980, pp. 11–16. Also see Fathi Osman, *Sharia in Contemporary Society,* Los Angeles 1994, pp. 18–33; Muddathir 'Abd al Rahim, *The Development of Fiqh in the Modern Muslim World,* Kuala Lumpur 1996, p. 2,3; Khaled Abou El Fadl, *The Authoritative and Authoritarian in Islamic Discourses,* Los Angeles 1997.

practically no aspect of human life that is not subject to the law. Islamic law represents an order which governs all spheres of life, in which, as found otherwise only in Mosaic law, even the rules of protocol and etiquette are of a legal nature.[4] As a result, it is impossible to differentiate clearly between Muslim theologians and lawyers. The fact that theology and jurisprudence are equated means that Islam as a belief and civilization, a religion and culture, cannot be understood without an understanding of Islamic jurisprudence.

The comprehensive character of *al fiqh* is illustrated very well by compendia of Islamic law, whose first chapters are usually devoted to the rules and formalities for prayer.[5]

In contrast to Western legal systems Islamic jurisprudence does not make a distinction in principle between:

*   law and equity,
*   public and private law,
*   procedural law and substantive law,
*   criminal law and torts,
*   law of conflicts (international private law) and the law of nations (international law).

Superficially, therefore, descriptions of Islamic law seems to suffer from insufficient analytical efforts.

Of course the first and main source of Islamic law is the Qur'an. However, the Qur'an contains only a small number of clear, normative rules, such as the prohibition of pork and of gambling; some of these rules are ambiguous—such as the prohibition of *ribā* (interest) which requires a definition of 'usury'; others are clothed in the form of recommendations or dissuasions, without threat of punishment in this world (regarding homosexuality, for example).[6]

---

4. See Yusuf al-Qaradawi, *The Lawful and the Prohibited in Islam,* Kuwait 1989; see also Ernst Klingmüller, "Recht und Religion—Einige Gedanken zum Werden und Wesen des Rechts im Islam," in *Gottes ist der Orient—Gottes ist der Okzident, Festschrift für A. Falaturi,* Cologne 1990, pp. 47 ff.

5. Examples of this include al Nawawi, *Minhaj al Talibin,* Lahore 1977; Abdur Rahman I. Doi, *Shari'ah: The Islamic Law,* London 1984; Said Ramadan, *Das islamische Recht,* Wiesbaden 1979; Ahmad ibn Naqib al Misri, *The Reliance of the Traveller; A Classic Manual of Islamic Sacred Law,* amana publications, Beltsville, MD 1997; Ibn Rushd, *The Distinguished Jurist's Primer (Bidāyat al Mujtahid),* 2 vol., Reading, U.K., 1994, 1996.

6. The nuanced legal quality of Qur'anic norms has been well worked out in Abdoldjavad Falaturi, "Die Saria—das islamische Rechtssystem," in *Weltmacht Islam,* Munich 1988.

Even if we neglected the fact that each and every verbal statement is subject to, indeed requires, interpretation, the Prophet's understanding of the Qur'an would clearly be of decisive importance. This, the Prophet's traditions (his Sunnah), his understanding of the Qur'an contained in Hadith collections, is the second source of Islamic law.[7] Whether this is also true of traditions which can be traced back not to the Prophet, but to first generation companions only, is rightly controversial.

This second legal source is, incidentally, anchored in the Qur'an where God orders that Muslims follow the Prophet.[8] Thus, everything he said, did or tolerated became an ethical or moral example at the very least, and in many cases a standard to emulate faithfully. (This explains why a reading of the Qur'an alone is not adequate for an understanding of the phenomenon of Islam.) Later generations naturally had to look out for additional legal answers, arrived at mainly through drawing on analogies, because questions inevitably arose to which neither Qur'an nor Sunnah offered ready answers. It was, however, not only permitted to solve new cases by analogy, but also to develop the law further by elaborating a scholarly consensus, rare as that might be. The Qur'an's promise that:

You are indeed the best community brought about for mankind: you order what is right and forbid what is wrong and believe in God. (3:110)

was understood as a guarantee that the Muslim community as a whole would never err on important issues simultaneously.

Thus, it is clear that Islamic law remained flexible enough to take into account the requirements of 'public interest,' but that it was also vulnerable to the re-integration of some pre-Islamic customs. Nevertheless, Islamic jurisprudence to this day refuses to be receptive to the concepts of 'natural law,' 'customary law' and 'law of equity'.

But what is more important, Islamic law also rejects legislation as a legal source, i.e., bills of law enacted by parliament. Its view is that laws cannot be promulgated, only found within the realm of Revelation, thanks to one or other of the four legal sources and methods sketched above.

---

7. The most accessible and reliable ones are *Sahīh al Bukhārī*, Chicago, 9 vols, 1976; *Sahīh Muslim,* Lahore, 4 vols, 1976; Imam Malik, *al Muwatta,* London 1982; in extracts: Muh. Asad, *Sahīh al Bukhārī*, Gibraltar 1981; Muh. Rassoul, *Sahīh al Bukhārī,* Cologne 1989; *Riyādh us Sālihīn,* collected by Imam al Nawawi, Munich 1996 (in German).
8. 2:30; 4:59.

Thus, early Islamic legal scholars had an enormous responsibility and power, far beyond that which a European jurist has ever had, even if it often landed them in jail; their power was comparable only to the role of a judge in the U.S. Supreme Court. This phenomenon can still be observed today; for example, in the way in which legal advice (*fatwā*) issued by the Great Shaykh al Azhar, President of the al Azhar University in Cairo, on contemporary issues like surrogate motherhood gains general acceptance.

In spite of this, following the Western model, the Ottoman Empire with its 'Mecelle' Civil Code of 1877 started the process of codifying Muslim law. Since then the legislative machine in all Islamic countries except Saudi Arabia has been working overtime; still, Muslim legislators usually emphasize that all legislation which does not conform with the Qur'an is either automatically null and void or must be amended at the earliest opportunity.

However, no true Muslim has ever dared to attempt a codification of the *shari'ah* as such—except in subsidiary areas such as family law (for example, in Algeria and Morocco).[9] The leap from the collection and systematization of case law to codification, as was ventured in American law on the basis of private 'Restatements of the Law,' is consciously avoided in Islam because any codification would inevitably cement particular interpretations and because every abstraction is, of course, reductionist and (most likely) minimalist.

Codification would also assume that an exhaustive list of Qur'anic norms could be made—and that is impossible. No one can predict which verse might one day become decisive in a new context. Also every verse of the Qur'an should always be read in context of the whole book; it may not be isolated—not even in the form of a legal codification.

In the Islamic world legal compendia by great professors can achieve legal authority even today merely by virtue of their prestige. However, this phenomenon of professorial law has a negative aspect: the extreme fictionality of Islamic law. The ideal, as represented by legal scholars, and legal reality, as practiced by various Caliphs, Vizirs, Sultans and Emirs, diverged widely soon after the early years of Islam. Islamic law was, therefore, often more of a mirror to be held before the ruler and not the ideal that he applied.

Legal scholars themselves contributed to this regrettable development when they advised in favor of almost total obedience, even to sinful or

---

9. *Al Mudawwanah,* amended in 1993.

barely legitimate rulers, for reasons of State, as occurred already in the dispute between 'Ali and Mu'awīyah. Muslim scholars in the Sunni world tended to value stability higher than justice.

For this reason the legal sphere in the Islamic world, to this day, remains characterized by a dualism: the idealistic domain of legal scholars and the uglier side of reality. Islamic law has only rarely controlled the State; the Islamic State has never controlled the law.

Not much has changed in most countries where the majority of Muslims live today; this is the background to the passionate plea to 'introduce the shari'ah,' which echoes from Indonesia to the Maghrib.

Great significance is attached to the fact that in Sunni Islam four legal schools have been formed during the course of Islamic legal history—the Mālikī, Ḥanafī, Shāfi'ī, and Ḥanbalī 'rites'—in addition to the schools of the Shi'ah (the Twelvers and the Zaydis) and the 'Ibadites. This was never a symptom of factionalism, but proof of the liveliness and tolerance of the truly pluralistic intellectual life in Islam, as characterized by strong academic personalities—Abū Ḥanīfah (died 767), Mālik b. Anas (died 795), Muhammad b. Idris al Shāfi'ī (died 820) and Ahmad b. Ḥanbal (died 855)—none of whom had ever intended to found a 'school'. In those days legal interpretations differed so widely that adherence to a specific school might, in certain cases, make the difference between life and death.

Meanwhile, a dialectic process has led to such a close rapprochement that it no longer seemed utopian when, in 1989, King Hasan II of Morocco called for work to bring about a unified legal rite, at least for all Sunni Muslims.

That a Tunisian belongs to the school of Imam Malik would only be obvious today by the fact that his Egyptian or Turkish neighbor does not let his arms hang by his sides at prayer but, instead, crosses them over his chest. Nor should it obstruct fusion that Shafi'i Muslims start their morning prayer (*salat al fajr*) earlier than others.

Legal alignment within the Sunni schools is, however, only conceivable if a rapprochement were to be reached between the rigorous, fundamentalist Ḥanbali school in its Saudi-Wahhabi form and the other schools. This does not seem likely unless such alignment were to be brought about by the sheer growth of fundamentalism (see the chapter "Fundamentalism").

The main problem of legal unification is linked to a framework of criteria common to all schools. All conceivable actions and omissions are judged by Muslims according to the five categories of

• permitted/forbidden,

- recommended/not recommended, and
- optional or indifferent.

In addition, there is consensus that

- anything which has not been expressly forbidden is to be regarded as permitted,[10]
- the intention is decisive for the moral value of an action,[11]
- the impossible cannot be a duty,[12] and
- in cases of doubt it is better to avoid an action which is ambivalent in nature.

A problematic trend arose at an early stage and is primarily discernable today among the 'Ibadite Mozabites in Algeria and the Wahhabis in Saudi Arabia, in which the categories 'recommended/not recommended' are progressively eliminated. These puritan Muslims of Algeria and Saudi Arabia tend to regard everything recommended as obligatory and anything not recommended as prohibited, an innovation which, since it is 'pious', is regarded as permissible (bid'ah ḥasanah).

The result of this innovation certainly corresponds to the ascetic's ideal of imitating the Prophet as he strives towards saintliness (in the Christian sense). Yet this puritanical, pietist stance leads Islam—the religion of the middle way and of moderation—along the path of a rigoristic élite and, therefore, away from a universal religion within reach of the average person, who is no scoundrel, but no Sufi either.

Moves have been made in this direction throughout Islamic history. We only have to recall the Berber Almoravids (al Murabiṭūn) and Almohads (al Muwaḥḥidūn) active in North Africa and Spain from the 11th to the 13th century and today's supporters of the Front du Salut Islamique (FIS) in Algeria, a development which can lead to the point of hostility toward amenities of life, banishing all joy from it. In my opinion this is not in accordance with the aim of the liberating message of the Qur'an, when it appealed to Muslims to pray for good in this life and not only for good in the Afterlife: āṭīnā fi al dunyā ḥasanah wa fi al ākhirah ḥasanah (2:201).

It is for this reason that we should insist on respect for the principle that what God has not forbidden is allowed, and no one should dare to curtail this freedom:

---

10. 5:87, 16:116.
11. 33:5; Hadith no. 1 from Ezzedin Ibrahim and Denys Johnson-Davies, al Nawawi, Forty Hadith, Damascus 1976.
12. 2:286; 6:152; 7:42; 23:62.

> **O you who believe! Do not forbid yourselves the good things which**
> **God has made lawful for you . . . (5:87)**

What then, against this background, does the call to 'introduce the shari'ah' mean if it is more than a political slogan?

In the narrow sense, we may understand the introduction of the shari'ah to mean that the Qur'an becomes the supreme constitution of a State, that is the highest standard against which all laws, including the written constitution are measured, so that it is possible in Muslim countries for there to be *unconstitutional constitutional* law.

This is demanded by even the most moderate Muslims.

However, in many quarters introduction of the shari'ah is demanded in a more comprehensive sense, namely, as a sizeable body of law to be directly applied in all spheres, which leaves no room for codification by the State. This would mean the introduction of a legal system—not only Qur'anic penal law—very close to the original Islamic ideal, more or less as practiced today in Saudi Arabia. (The Kingdom treats Qur'an and Sunnah as its constitution, its family, inheritance, and penal law.) Muslims who advocate this are, however, usually unclear about the exact point in the history of Islamic law they wish to return to with the application of the shari'ah. Alas, we may assume that many are thinking of the legal system as it had congealed in about the fifteenth century, when the unfortunate notion of 'closing the doors' on responsible new interpretations (*ijtihad*) had already led to a paralysis of the system. This would be a fundamentalism which comes to a halt a long distance from the foundations.

HUMAN RIGHTS

The Western world is quite rightly proud of its human rights history, a history which, from the Stoics onwards, seems to have taken place almost exclusively in the Christian cultural sphere. Indeed, the milestones of this development:

- the Magna Charta libertatum of 1215,
- the Habeas Corpus Act of 1679,
- the British Bill of Rights of 1698,
- the American Declaration of Independence of 1776, and
- the French Declaration of Human and Civil Rights of 1789

are now part of the general knowledge of every halfway educated person.

Psychologically, this has far-reaching consequences. On the one hand it is commonly assumed that Western legal development as it stands could claim universal validity; on the other, one frequently encounters Western legal experts who regard the legal history of the rest of the world, especially the Islamic one, as barbaric, despite the fact that they know nothing about it.

This explains the triumphal march of the, in actual fact non-binding, Universal Declaration of Human Rights of the United Nations of 10 December 1948 and the two International Pacts of 19 December 1966 on (a) civil and political and (b) economic, social and cultural rights, which were also ratified by many Muslim States.

The fact that this was not an unbroken line of development is often overlooked, despite the fact that these breaks could bring about the collapse of the entire edifice of human rights.

The first and probably most important break took place between the American Declaration of Independence and the French declaration of human rights (*Déclaration des droits de l'homme et du citoyen*) only a few years later; for the fathers of the American revolution traced back to *God* the 'truths' or rights which they regarded as 'self-evident'. The French Jacobins, however, understood human rights only in terms of natural rights (*droits naturels*) as *agreed* upon.

With this the axe was already laid against the future edifice of human rights. For it can only be stable if fundamental rights are understood, in agreement with the Islamic view, as rights laid down by God, not *created* by man, but simply *discovered* or recognized by him as already and eternally existing.

At the end of the day respect for human rights stands or falls with the belief in God. Those who deny Him involuntarily place all rights at the mercy of human disposition, even if they deceive themselves by referring to putative 'natural rights'. No one has ever been able to derive a concrete and generally convincing legal system from the contemplation of nature. In fact, those who try only project their own ideological ideas onto 'nature'. In these cases the real validity of the law is actually founded not in nature but in convention, in a social consensus (*contrat social*).

The results speak for themselves: the signing of human rights pacts and declarations by no means led to an improvement in the legal protection of the individual in atheist countries, especially in the Communist world.

The second break came from the development of human rights conceived as demands on the State. As is well-known, the formulation of classical human rights in past centuries aimed at the curtailment of State power only, by giving the citizen freedom from something or liberty to do something. The State, reined in by a bill of rights, was to be prevented from taxing, arresting, dispossessing or executing at will. The accent was not on what the State should *do,* but on what it should *not* do. Recently, however, human rights have been formulated in terms of demands for welfare State action. The State should guarantee employment, housing, health care, even the enjoyment of the natural world and the happiness of the individual. This has led to an inflation of 'human rights' and to an inflation of the State sector. Both perversions can be equally dangerous for the survival of the lofty ideal of human rights as the loss of transcendental links.

At any rate, true human rights are discredited when, for example, we hear talk of a 'fundamental right' to feel afraid (e.g., of nuclear war) or to drug oneself. Even more absurd 'fundamental rights' will probably follow.

Islam refuses to go along with such fad and folly, and yet is one of the earliest and most comprehensive classical human rights systems in the world.

For Muslims every right deserving that name must be traceable back to divine sources—the Qur'an and the Sunnah of the Prophet.

Islamic jurisprudence is exemplary in its insistence that fundamental rights cannot be created by man but can only be brought to light by him.

Thus, human rights have found their most solid foundation of all in Islamic legal theory.

Despite this, human rights do not occupy a particularly prominent position, even in contemporary Islamic legal literature;[1] indeed, as a rule they are not even regarded as a specific category of rights.[2]

But it would be wrong to conclude that there is, therefore, insufficient legal protection in this sphere. The theoretical underexposure of human rights is a result of the traditional system of compiling Islamic law. Since all laws based on the Qur'an being equally divine have the same status, Muslim literature usually does not deal with 'human rights' as a specific group, but rather, in the context of various subjects—marital law, criminal law, economic law. Textbook chapters on the rights of aliens come closest to Western systematics.

Furthermore, Islamic law differs in that it takes into account that all rights whatsoever, including human rights, are only guaranteed in reality if the entire social and legal system is in good shape, i.e., that the noble aim of justice can only be realized as a by-product of a comprehensive and just social system, and not in isolation

More important than systematics is the substance: the question of whether Islam in theory, if not in fact, guarantees human rights.

Fortunately, there are no major differences between the Western and the Islamic perception of the ideal relationship between citizen and State. On the basis of the Qur'an, the following fundamental rights are guaranteed: life, corporal inviolability, liberty, equal treatment/nondiscrimination, property, freedom of conscience, marriage, legal hearing, the assumption of innocence, *nulla poena sine lege* (no punishment without prior threat of punishment), protection from torture, and asylum.

---

1. Islamic initiatives for an Islamic human rights declaration or a model constitution for an Islamic State have until now had no decisive success; see, for example, *A Model of an Islamic Constitution,* Islamabad, 10 December 1983; see also the "General Declaration of Human Rights" of the so-called Islamic Council for Europe of 1981 and the "Declaration of Human Rights in Islam" passed by the Organization of the Islamic Conference (OIC) on 5 August 1990 in Cairo, printed in *CIBEDO,* Frankfurt 1991, pp. 178 ff.

2. See amongst others Joseph Schacht, *An Introduction to Islamic Law,* Oxford 1964; Said Ramadan, *Das islamische Recht,* Wiesbaden 1979; Abdur Rahman I. Doi, *Shari'ah: The Islamic Law,* London 1984; Isam K. Salem, *Islam und Völkerrecht,* Berlin; Hans Kruse, *Islamische Völkerrechtslehre,* 2nd edition, Bochum 1979; Abu A'la Mawdudi, *Human Rights in Islam,* Leicester, U.K., 1976; *Conferences of Riyad, Paris, Vatican City, Geneva, and Strasbourg on Moslem Doctrine and Human Rights in Islam,* Riyad (n.d.).

All this has been legally guaranteed for 1400 years now.[3]

Above all, in this context the differences to the Western human rights codex are of interest.

These may be reduced to a few points:

1. The human rights pacts, including the European Human Rights Convention of 4 November 1950, contain formulations on the equality of men and women, in particular, before the law and in marriage, which Muslim States can only ratify with reservations. Islamic law does not discriminate against women when comparing them to men, in as much as that which is different may be treated differently and only that which is the same must be treated the same. And this is the crux of the matter: for Western theory simply denies the legal relevance of differences between men and women, while Islam refuses to go along with this fiction (see the chapter "Woman in Society").

2. According to Islamic law the right to change one's religion without legal disadvantages does not exist for a Muslim. At the very least his conversion to another religion would have consequences regarding inheritance and possibly marriage (invalidation of his marriage with a Muslim woman), even though there is certainly no Qur'anic command to execute renegades.[4] This situation will be easily understood if to be a Muslim is equated with *citizenship* in a Western country. Nobody denies there that certain privileges and special duties are linked to the possession of citizenship.

3. Non-Muslim citizens in Islamic States do not have equal access to political office, but only in so far as they are denied the office of head of State. (In this respect, a non-Muslim, incidentally, is no worse off than an American citizen born abroad who cannot present himself in U.S. presidential elections.)

4. Since judicial mistakes—a miscarriage of justice—cannot be corrected in cases of capital punishment many countries would like to see the death penalty abolished world-wide, not least because it was abused a hundred thousand times during the Nazi period and in the Communist world. But the Islamic world has not joined them

---

3. Most astounding in Qur'anic law are perhaps the detailed regulations for the self-adjudication, and religious freedom of minorities—evidence of the profound tolerance of Islam. See Muddaththir 'Abd al Rahim, *Islam and Non-Muslim Minorities*, Penang, Malaysia 1997.

4. In the Middle Ages apostates were often treated like traitors during war and therefore executed in accordance with 5:33.

because the Qur'an allows death penalty for three offenses—high treason, murder, and robbery. There is no obligation to carry out such punishment regardless of circumstances, yet a general deletion of the death penalty from the books is not possible in Islamic States.

5. A similar, thank God only formal problem, is represented by slavery, despised the world over, because it was tolerated at the time by the Qur'an as part of the existing martial law. Enslaved non-Muslim prisoners of war became bondsmen with concrete rights and duties, not reified true slaves according to Roman law, who could be treated like chattels.

However, in many a surah of the Qur'an God suggested that the liberation of servants taken prisoners of war was a particularly deserving act. The Qur'an itself therefore paved the way for the abolition of slavery.

Although it appears that pockets of slavery continue to surface in some parts of the world—as may be concluded from its periodic official abolition in Mauritania—no serious Muslim would today wish to maintain this historical institution—overcome at God's wish—except in order to preserve the text of the Qur'an integrally.

Since God described it as a good deed to free slaves, and since it has been *de facto* abolished anyway, it should at least be permissible today to renounce slavery contractually, as in Article 8 of the UN Declaration of Human Rights and Article 4 of the International Pact of civil and political rights.

Thus, there is really no essential contradictions—certainly no cultural clash—between the Islamic and the Western human rights doctrines. On the contrary: Islam is a (complementary) human rights system.

Alas, Muslims have reasons to believe that many in the West have a vested interest in "perpetuating the damaging myth that Islam and human rights are incompatible,"[5] and that the Occident will continue to use human rights as a political weapon against Muslim countries while itself—witness Bosnia!—being deplorably selective in honoring them.

---

5. Neil Hicks, "Islam and Human Rights," *Muslim Politics Report* no. 12 (March/April) 1997, pp. 1,4,5.

WOMAN IN SOCIETY

In his sensitive and poetic biography of the Prophet, *La vie de Mahomet,* Virgil Gheorghiu describes the significance of women for desert Arabs in the following manner:

> For an Arab a woman has an importance as nothing else on earth . . . The only soft line found in the desert, corresponding to the trees of a fruit garden, these are the outlines of the female form.
>
> In the desert women replace the garden, the flowers, the aromatic fruits, the blue, winding rivers, the fast-flowing streams and the bubbling of the springs ... Woman in the desert is all the beauty and all the splendor of the universe, condensed into one body.[1]

Is it conceivable that this people despised women before it became Islamic?

In all its 114 chapters (*sūrahs*), none of which is dedicated to men, the Qur'an contains one, the fourth, which is not only called "The Women" (*al Nisā'*), but deals in detail with women's rights and their family lives.

The first verse of this *sūrah* underlines the essential similarity and equal value of man and woman:

> **O people! Be conscious of your Lord, who created you out of a single living being and created out of it its mate, and from these two spread countless men and women.**

The Qur'an, unambiguous and coherent, applies to women and men equally. According to the Qur'an, both sexes share a common fate, and are subject to the same existential conditions, with the same spiritual potential and the same purpose of being.

Is it conceivable that this religion justifies regulations which are hostile to women ?

Without doubt, women played a major role in the life of the Prophet of Islam, and were held in the highest esteem by him. Even Muslim femi-

---

1. Virgil Gheorghiu, *La vie de Mahomet,* Paris 1970.

nists such as Fatimah Mernissi accept this.[2] The love affair of Muhammad and his young, highly talented wife 'Ā'ishah is widely known. What is less well-known is the fact that Muhammad was monogamously and happily married to his first wife Khadījah for 24 years, until her death. She was 15 years his elder and, incidentally, had asked for his hand in marriage. And the fact is that the other marriages concluded by the Prophet as head of State in Madinah were primarily of dynastic importance and thus political or even humanitarian in nature.[3]

Is it conceivable that such a man should want to give his message a misogynist character?

Yet there is no greater obstacle to the spread of Islam in the Western world than the stereotype conviction, which has become a cliché, that Muslim women are prevented from developing their personality, chained to the kitchen sink, stifled and enslaved.

But there is no smoke without fire. No one would deny that the position and role of women has become problematic in the Islamic world, too, despite the fact that Islam originally improved the status of the Arab woman considerably from some unscrupulous traditions of the (pre-Islamic) 'time of ignorance,' the *Jāhilīyah*.

A flood of modern Islamic publications on the subject reflects this new awareness of the problem.[4] However, when dealing with this difficult issue we must differentiate between:

---

2. Fatima Mernissi, *Women and Islam: An Historical and Theological Inquiry,* Oxford 1991.

3. According to the Qur'an 33:50, the Prophet was allowed to marry more than four women; he had 15 in all, virtually all—after 'Ā'ishah—former widows. It happened that Muhammad, after a battle, would quickly espouse a women from the subdued tribe in order to save all prisoners from being enslaved.

4. See above all the *Index of Islamic Literature of the Islamic Foundation* in Leicester, Great Britain, which appears four times a year with the *Muslim World Book Review;* of modern German literature, I refer here only to articles in *Al Islam* (Munich):

Aischa Lemu, "Die Frau im Islam," nos. 3,4,5/1988 and no. 1/1989;

Fatima Grimm, "Das Familienleben im Islam," no. 3/1989;

Asiye Zilelioglu, "Köhler, Eine Chance für Frauen," no. 4/1986.

In English literature:

Abdur Rahman I. Doi, *Women in Shar'iah,* Nigeria 1983;

Fathi Osman, "Muslims and Personal Law in India," *Arabia* (London) March 1986;

Faith & Freedom—Women's Human Rights in the Muslim World, ed. Mahnaz Afkhami, London/NY 1995.

Anon, 'The ancient rights of Muslim women," *Arabia,* July 1985, p. 78;

In French literature:

Rabah Stambouli, "La femme en Islam," *Al Moujahid,* Algiers, 2./3 February 1990; "La femme et le Coran," *HORIZONS,* Algiers, 9 / 10 March 1990.

- Islamic and general phenomena,
- Islam as a religion and Islam as a civilization,
- Religious theory versus religious practice.

As a starting-point we should accept the fact that women are still discriminated against in the workplace all over the world. As Sylvia Ann Hewlett ascertained in her book *A Lesser Life: The Myth of Women's Liberation in America* (1986), women in the USA then still earned a mere 64 percent of men's salaries and even in Sweden the figure is only 81 percent.

Just as universal is the cult of boys, expressly condemned in the Qur'an (16:58 f). After all, female births are not valued any more highly in China, India or in the Christian Latin world than in the Arab world. It is a cult which, curiously enough, women themselves perpetuate.

Furthermore, it is easy to see that appearance and role of woman vary considerably within the Islamic world, thus revealing to be in part culturally determined. We need only consider the traditions regarding the 'covering' of women, which vary from country to country, and within earch country from countryside to town. Therefore it cannot be denied that inspite of the pro-women policy of the Prophet, pre-Islamic misogynist attitudes soon reappeared, as from the Caliphate of 'Umar ibn al Khattab. Some of that remains alive even today in the form of an Arab machismo cult of jealousy.[5]

It is, therefore, necessary to isolate precisely the few, truly Islamic aspects of the status of Muslim women.

We are dealing here with elements concerning
- marriage
- family life
- divorce
- dress
- inheritance law
- testimony in court,

each of which are dealt with below.

Marriage

In contrast to a man, a previously unmarried Muslim woman may give her assent to marriage silently, although the Roman law principle of *qui*

---

5. See Mernissi, *loc. cit.* For an overview over all issues discussed in this chapter see B. Aisha Lemu/Fatima Heeren, *Women in Islam,* Leicester 1978.

tacet consentire non videtur (silence is not assent) also applies in Islamic law. This is out of consideration for the assumed shyness and embarrassment of a young girl; it does not mean that a Muslim woman can be married against her will.

A female Muslim may only marry a male Muslim (60:10), but the Qur'an allows male Muslims to marry female Christians, and Jews and women of similar "people of the book" (5:5). This is the necessary consequence of the rules governing marriage in Islam in which the father is responsible for decisions regarding the upbringing of the older children. Thus, a Muslim woman would not be able to prevent her Christian husband from bringing up her children in the Christian faith.

And finally, a Muslim woman may only marry one husband, while men are allowed to marry up to four women, under certain conditions.

The rationale behind this regulation is manifold: amongst other things it has to do with the difficulty of determining paternity—*pater semper incertus*, the Romans used to say.[6]

The above-mentioned conditions are such that polygyny[7] is usually ruled out under today's conditions. Indeed it has almost entirely disappeared in the Islamic world; therefore, it is possible to say that there is a built-in tendency towards monogamy in the Qur'an:

> **And if you fear that you cannot do justice toward the orphans, then marry from women who seem good to you, two or three or four. But if you fear that you will not be able to do justice—then only one ... (4:3)**

Polygyny, therefore, is only admitted under two conditions:
- if one can only do justice to orphans financially and psychologically through a further marriage, for example, by taking in a widowed sister-in-law with her children or by marrying an orphan girl;[8]
- if one can do equal justice to all wives, not only materially.[9]

On the latter point the Qur'an is quite clear and firm:

---

6. "Paternity is always uncertain."

7. *Polygeny* is the practice of having more than one wife. This is habitually called *polygamy* which, however, strictly speaking means having either more than one wife or more than one husband.

8. Needless to say that this condition has been interpreted in great variety.

9 This latter condition presupposes that the first wife had not excluded a second marriage in the marriage contract.

And you are never able to treat your wives with equal fairness, however much you may desire it . . . (4:129)

Time and again God warns polygenous husbands against self-deception with the remark: **"God knows what is on your minds!"**[10]

Whoever heeds this must come to the conclusion that polygyny, as practiced in the past at the courts of the great and small—caliphs, sultans emirs, and viziers—has never been sanctioned by the Qur'an, but has always been arbitrary, inhuman and therefore un-Islamic.

One is further forced to ascertain that polygyny of the ordinary man, if at all, can only be justified in borderline cases, that is, only if there is an exceptional need for it and that the women concerned are psychologically prepared for it. This may be the case, for example, if—as after the Second World War—the loss of men was so horrendous that large numbers of young women of a given generation had no chance of marriage without polygyny. It is also conceivable that a woman on her way to dying of cancer should want a second woman in the household: to take care of her, to become accustomed to the children, and to ensure the future of the family. And it is not only conceivable, but a reality, that there are modern, intellectual women, brought up in the Western way—as, for example, the American Maryam Jameela who converted from Judaism to Islam—who feel comfortable in a polyganous marriage, which they have actively sought.

At any rate, polygyny is no longer regarded as immoral without admitting exception, even by German courts of law.[11]

In sum, it would not only be inadmissible, but short-sighted to dismiss the institution of polygyny out of hand.

Family life

Legal systems throughout the world have to face the problem of what to do when marriage partners disagree on how to conduct family affairs in this or that respect. After all, a majority decision is impossible. There are only two possible solutions: either one of the two partners is generally, or in certain cases, given the power to decide (which amounts to a veto power)—this is the Islamic solution—or the argument is taken out-

---

10. Qur'an 5:7; 11:5; 39:7; 57:6; 67:13.

11. See *Frankfurter Allgemeine Zeitung,* 3 May 1985, p. 7. "Zweite Frau nicht sittenwidrig" (Second wife not amoral), for a decision of the Supreme Federal Administrative Court in Berlin, file no. AZ 1 c, 33.81.

side the family for arbitration or decision by the extended family, the registry office or the court. This has become the Western way, with the absurd result that, for a time, German clerks literally had to throw dice on which family name to give to the wife if the spouses could not agree.

Islam has opted clearly in favor of taking decisions on family affairs inside the family and, as a rule, gives the husband—normally the provider and protector—the decisive vote. God says in the Qur'an: **"Men shall take full care of women," because God has given the one more (strength) than the other, and because they support them.**[12]

This does not limit the mother's prerogative of caring and deciding for the smaller children nor her exclusive right to manage and dispose of her personal property, including her dowry. In this respect, for 1400 years Muslim women have enjoyed the advantages of a complete separation of property between husband and wife, while most European women have been liberated from the administration by their husbands of their personal property only since the mid-twentieth century, if at all.

Islam regards a woman's calling to motherhood to be her most noble and most fulfilling task and the basis for her particular dignity and for her self-realization as a creative personality in the fullest sense. This high regard for motherhood is expressed in the Prophet's famous statement that Paradise is found at the feet of the mothers.

Is it not significant that the shari'ah foresees a severe penalty for the slandering of honorable women—the false accusation of adultery (24:4ff.)?

Muslims are, however, of the opinion that—even in cases of adultery or rape—the life of the foetus is not at the disposition of a prospective mother, even if "her belly belongs to her," as feminists would say. The Qur'an does not reject birth control or family planning, for reasons of personal, social or national necessity, but it does reject abortion (17:33). In fact, there are no Islamic 'pro-life' and 'pro-choice' lobbies.[13]

---

12. 4:34. It would be wrong to read into this statement of principle any superiority of men over women. Verse 4:34 does not deal with questions of status but with practical issues of maintenance and protection.

13. Abortion is not mentioned in the Qur'an, but must be regarded as prohibited from the moment of conception onwards because it destroys life. From around the 120th day of pregnancy abortion is particularly abhorrent because at this stage in development a human being endowed with a soul has been formed (Qur'an 23:12–14); Abdullah Borek, *Deutsche Muslim Liga,* Rundbrief 06/92; Yusuf al Qaradawi, *The Lawful and the Prohibited in Islam,* Kuwait, 1989, p. 172 f. For all reproductive issues see Hassan Hathout, M.D., *Reading the Muslim Mind,* Plainfield, Indiana, 1995, in particular pp. 123–125; "Islam and Family Planning," *Proceedings of the International Islamic Conference in Rabat, December 1971,* London 1986.

Islam does not see marriage as a sacrament. Indeed, it does not differ-entiate between the sacred and the secular. Marriage is, however, regard-ed as a form of worship in Islam, a religious duty for everyone able to afford it. Muslims regard monasticism and celibacy on religious grounds as an aberration, reflecting misinterpretations of earlier divine messages.

In Islam, too, marriage is meant to be permanent. Temporary marriages (*mut'ah*) concluded for a limited period, are accepted in Shi'ah school of fiqh only. Thus, marriage is a vital institution Islam tries to protect. This aim explains the absolute prohibition of sexual relationships outside mar-riage (17:32), the disapproval of homosexuality (7:81; 27:55), the dis-couragement of divorce, as well as the dress regulations for men and women described in the chapter "The Veiled Orient".

Safeguarding of marriage is also the rationale behind the frequently abused and mostly misunderstood Qur'anic provision, according to which a husband may 'beat' his wife. It does read:

As for those women from whom you have reason to fear desertion, (first) admonish them, (then) refuse to share their beds and (final-ly) beat them. (4:34)

The Islamic tradition agrees that this rule is designed to save a marriage in trouble, thereby forestalling the danger of immediate irreparable divorce in anger. After all, according to another famous saying of the Prophet, divorce is the most detestable of all actions allowed by God. With this in mind, there is general agreement among Muslims from the earliest times that 'beating' may only take the form of a gesture—such as a symbolic slap with a fan or a towel—definitely without the intent to inflict physical injury. Any other reaction would be counter productive—destroying, rather than preserving the threatened bond of marriage. The Prophet personally rejected *any* corporal punishment of his wives.[14]

Divorce

In marital situations from which there is no other way out, divorce remains permissible as a necessary escape valve and is available for both marriage partners, the only difference being in the procedures. Divorce initiated by the man (*talāq*) is easier in terms of procedure. Divorce becomes final if unilaterally pronounced by the husband over a period of

14. See in greater detail Muhammad Asad, *The Message of the Qur'an*, Gibraltar 1980, note 45 to Qur'an 4: 34. The Prophet's attitude should be considered morally binding.

three months. This takes into account that with the divorce he forfeits the
entire, possibly very large amount of money (*al mahar*) he had to give his
wife before marriage. If wives were also able to leave marriage so easily,
it could encourage a systematic misappropriation of the marriage gift. For
this reason a court must decide on a contested divorce initiated by the
wife (*khul'*).

Inheritance

Qur'anic inheritance law provides for the inheritance of brothers and
sisters in case their parents die (4:7), with the sister only inheriting half
of her brother's share (4:11). The rationale behind this is the duty of male
heirs to take sole financial responsibility for the maintenance of the entire
family. Unequal responsibilities justify unequal claims.

Testimony in Court

Finally, there is one more case in which Muslim women may not treated in the same way as men, and that is when they appear as witnesses in
court. As a rule, Islamic law demands that a fact should be corroborated
by two witnesses, but the evidence of two women is equated to that of one
man (2:282).[15] Today, Islamic scholars wonder whether the rationale
behind this rule is rooted in physical conditions to which women are temporarily subject (i.e., cyclical strains including premenstrual syndromes;
post-natal depression; menopausal effects) or whether it takes account of
the normal infamiliarity of housewives with business matters and procedures. If so, the evidence of a business woman should be considered equal
to any male evidence. At any rate, scholars agree today that it would be
utterly wrong to infer from *al Baqarah* (2):282 any natural ethical or
intellectual difference between the two genders.

These then are the specific conditions for the development of Muslim
women, conditions that did not prevent many of them from playing a historical role. The history of these 'ladies of Islam' is still to be written,
despite Fatima Mernissi's attempts[16] It might begin with 'Ā'ishah, who
reliably transmitted the text of the Qur'an orally as well as a significant
number of relevant personal memories of the Prophet, but who also acted
as an epoch-making politician and even as a military commander during
'Ali's Caliphate. Such a history would detail the lives of Rābi'ah al
'Adawīyah, the great mystic of Baṣrah (c. 713–801) and of some of the

---

15. Al Nawawi, *Manual of Muhammadan Law*, Lahore 1977, p. 517; Shamshad M.
Khan, *Why Two Women Witnesses??*, London 1993; Anwar Ahmad Qadrī, *Islamic
Jurisprudence in the Modern World*, Lahore 1981.

16. Fatima Mernissi, *Sultanes Oubliées—Femmes Chefs d'Etat en Islam*, Casablanca
1990.

Caliphs' wives who, like Umm Salamah and Aruya, greatly influenced their husbands intellectually or who, like Khayzaran and Shajarat al Durr, took over the regency for a time themselves.[17]

I fear, however, that this chapter on woman in Islam will be met with total incomprehension by some Western readers because it does not comply with the *zeitgeist*. After all, what part can a seemingly puritan code of sexual ethics play in a world without taboos, in which even sado-masochism, gay marriages, and sex with children are becoming widespread?

What is the use of praising marriage when more and more women are consciously deciding to become the 'single mothers'?

What effect can Islam have—with its condemnation of abortion—when the issue is no longer whether abortion is permissible, but only up to which month of pregnancy?

What use are dress codes in a time when even strip-tease series and hard-core pornography on television or video make over-saturated viewers yawn?

Of course Islam's scheme for life *is* from another world. It is an alternative that confronts the so-called modern world, its values, agnosticism, and 'anything goes' mentality, with a genuine counter-project that only appears to be outdated because it is timeless.

Timeless truths include the following facts:

- man and woman are biologically and therefore, both physically and psychologically different;
- the happiness of man and woman in their partnership is rooted in their polarity;
- adult love, but children too, find ideal conditions for development in only marriage conceived as a partnership; and
- unfettered sex can become destructive both for the individual and society.

It is therefore not surprising at all that we are already witnessing the casting of doubt on fashionable facets of the sexual and feminist revolution in the Western world. AIDS alone has forced people to rethink their manners in more than one respect. The first manageresses in the USA begin to express regret at their now irrevocable decision not to have children for the sake of their careers—at having placed too much emphasis on 'sisterhood' at the expense of 'motherhood'. More women than not are

---

17. op. cit.

now convinced that pure imitation of man is not the best way of liberating women. In the United States, as in Europe, it is once again fashionable among formerly 'swinging' students to 'go steady'.[18]

As early as 1968, in his prophetic book *Sexual Wilderness,* the American, Vance Packard, coined the term 'sex jungle' for the excesses of the sexual revolution in his country.

For me, the question is therefore not *whether* the pendulum will swing back to the center in this area too, but only *when* this will have occurred.

In short, Islam holds onto marriage and structures it around the natural role differentiation existing between men and women. For Islam, man and woman have the same dignity, but different tasks; they are of the same value, but have different abilities; they are equal before God, but have different roles in life. The question of whether or not this is modern is irrelevant.

Islam is not a fashion. It can wait.

18. See Hilton Kramer, "Die Angst vor dem Sex," *Frankfurter Allgemeine Zeitung,* 3 September 1986; John Leo, "Motherhood vs. Sisterhood," *TIME,* New York, 31 March 1986, p. 43; Sylvia Ann Hewlett, *A Lesser Life: The Myth of Women's Liberation in America,* New York 1986.

THE VEILED ORIENT

Despite the fact that the Western world has for centuries, on and on, fought wars with the Islamic world—in the Near East, the Balkans, Spain, North Africa, and the Caucasus—it has only sporadically, selectively, and tendentially shown interest for Islam as a religion and civilization. The sorry history of the translation of the Qur'an into European languages is symptomatic of this.

Nevertheless, even in the distant past there have been some individual attempts to understand the opposite world of ideas and learn from it, for example, by Francis of Assisi and Raymundus Lullus, and through the assimilation of Averroës or Avicenna. But by and large the image of Islam in the West remained grotesquely distorted until well into the nineteenth century.

The Orient remained veiled.

Then came the great era of the European orientalists who, since the last century, have been as busy as bees researching Islam, if not always with sympathy then with scientific passion. Hardly appreciated by Edward Said, the German contribution here has been of particularly high quality, and is associated with figures such as Carl Brockelmann, Heinz Halm, Alfred von Kremer, F. August Müller, Tilmann Nagel, Theodor Nöldecke (who dated the Qur'anic *surahs*), Rudi Paret, Friedrich Rückert (who translated the Qur'an into verse), Gustav Weil, Joseph Schacht, and Julius Wellhausen.

But French orientalists have also produced some excellent research. We need only think of scholars such as Jacques Berque, Régis Blachère, Claude Cahen, Henri Corbin, Louis Gardet and Henri Laoust.

Other nations have not been left out, as is testified by names such as Tor Andrae, Richard Bell, Frants Buhl, Ignaz Goldziher, Gustav von Grunebaum, Philip Hitti, Marshall G. S. Hodgeson, C. Snouk Hurgronje, P. J. Vatikiotis and William Montgomery Watt.

Not without distortions, this research has helped clarify the image of the Orient and of Islam in the West considerably and has also provided the Islamic world with important knowledge. Yet only a few Western orientalists have been capable of an emphatic observation of their subject on its own terms, so to speak from within.

Indeed, some, like Hamilton Gibb—not to speak of William Muir and David Samuel Margoliouth[1]—still viewed Islam through the spectacles of a Christian missionary, others such as Maxime Rodinson like a Marxist sociologist; some treated their rather disdained object of study in the manner of an ethnological researcher eager to analyze the primitive Muslim tribe quickly before it became extinct. Almost all consciously or unconsciously served the imperialistic penetration and subjugation of the Arab world, even though only few of them were, like T. E. Lawrence, true secret agents.

In 1978, Edward W. Said, Christian American of Palestinian origin, drew attention to this phenomenon in his bestseller *Orientalism*,[2] going so far as to compare anti-Arab orientalism with anti-Semitism. According to Said the 'Orient' is a European invention, the result of the projection of Eurocentric viewpoints and hidden European longings. He denounces the resulting 'orientalization of the Orient' as a manipulation to the advantage of European hegemonial politics. For example, even though the sensitive and pious Catholic researcher Louis Massignon personally identified with the Islamic mystic al Hallaj, it was only because Christian traits he had discovered in him.

Said has certainly uncovered more than a germ of truth, but has focused too sharply on ambiguous figures such as Richard Burton. At least since the twentieth century there have been Islamological and Oriental Studies which do not deal with the East purely in function with the Western supermodel, but is aware that cultural values may again travel from East to West, the dictum *ex oriente lux* (the light comes from the East) remain valid.

Such scholars, amongst whom I include not only European Muslims such as Leopold Weiss (Muhamad Asad), Titus Burckhardt, Ahmad von Denffer, Martin Lings, Roger du Pasquier and Mohamed Pickthall, but also 'sympathizers' such as Marcel Boisard, Henri Corbin, Daniel Gimaret, Neal Robinson, Sigrid Hunke, and Annemarie Schimmel have done more for the correction of the image of Islam than uneasy travelers between the two worlds such as Mohamed Arkoun[3] and Bassam Tibi who have come to sit between two stools.

---

1. Jabal Muhammad Buaben, *Image of the Prophet Muhammad in the West—A Study of Muir, Margoliouth and Watt*, Markfield (Leicester) 1995.
2. Edward Said, *Orientalism*, New York 1978; see also Karl Ulrich Syndram, "Der erfundene Orient in der europäischen Literatur . ." in *Europa und der Orient 800–1900*, Gütersloh 1989, p. 324.
3. Mohammed Arkoun, *Rethinking Islam*, Boulder, Colorado, 1994.

But it is still necessary for more books to be written such as *Allah ist ganz anders* (Allah is Quite Different)[4] if the Western mind is to be freed of his superior pose towards the Arab-Islamic world.

Despite excellent exhibitions such as "Europa und der Orient" (Europe and the Orient) in Berlin[5] in 1989, the Europeans' image of the Orient remains diffuse, by anything else determined by more than the suggestive atmosphere of stories from *Thousand and One Nights,*[6] which entertainment films, set anywhere in the Islamic world, continue to reflect: a mysterious, sensuous, unpredictable, fanatic, cruel, and above all, licentious Orient.

The veil which many Muslim women wear, in reality, does not fit in with this picture at all, in so far as it is an expression of a strictness of morals and sexual restraint that the West neither understands nor concedes to Islam. Veiling simply does not fit into the preconceived picture of the Islamic world. Rather it really reminds Europeans of the prudishness of Victorian times that they are used to ridiculing as stuffy.

And yet it is so. In the Islamic world, sexuality and affection are not displayed on the streets. Pornography is not tolerated. Girls wanting to get married normally refuse to enter into pre-marital relationships. Illegitimate children are a rarity. Most brides are virgins when they marry. Advertisements for wife-swapping, nudist beaches, homosexual bars, student communes—none of this exist in properly Muslim countries.

This is how old-fashioned Islam is—and it is proud of it.

Men's and women's dress, including the so-called veil (*ḥijāb*), reflects this; for from an Islamic point of view it is logical not to provoke what one does not wish to happen.

As far as covering the human body is concerned there is one basic consensus between Orient and Occident: both civilizations do not allow people, except infants, to walk around completely naked in everyday life. However, there is considerable difference regarding the extent of clothing thought necessary in public.

In the Islamic world itself, there is no uniform view on this matter, as a glance at the clothing of women in Morocco, Algeria, Tunisia, Anatolia,

---

4. Sigrid Hunke, "Allah ist ganz anders," *Enthüllungen von 1001 Vorurteilen über die Araber,* Bad König, 1990.

5. The 923-page catalogue for this exhibition (footnote 2) in Berlin-Keuzberg (28 May and 27 August 1989) documents many so far unrecognized influences of Islam on the development of art in the West.

6. *Alf Laylah wa Laylah,* fairy-tales and anecdotes of Indian-Persian origin, translated into Arabic during the 10th century and enriched with Arab material.

Egypt, Jordan, the Gulf States, Saudi Arabia, Pakistan, Malaysia, and Indonesia will confirm.

In Morocco, around half of all women and the great majority of those in towns, do not cover their hair; others veil even their faces. In Algeria, in 1990, most women covered their hair, some showing their faces, others wearing a piece of cloth over their nose and mouth, others showing only one eye. The Turkish peasant—like her sisters in the Christian mediterranean—retains her headscarf, but she would never contemplate veiling her face two or four-fold, as women in Saudi Arabian towns used to, at least before the Gulf War. In Indonesia, from her clothing alone, a Muslim woman can hardly be told apart from a Balinese woman. On the other hand, it is uncommon to meet a Muslim woman in Malaysia who does not cover her hair with a scarf.

Therefore, it is useful, especially against the background of the French 'war of the scarves' of 1989,[7] to examine the clothing rules of Qur'an and Sunnah found in the foremost three Qur'anic verses, namely in 33:53, 33:59 and 24:31.

The first of these regulations, known as *āyat al ḥijāb,* is concerned itself literally exclusively with the household of the Prophet. In this and only this very specific context it is ordered:

> **And whenever you ask them (i.e., his wives) for anything, ask them from behind a curtain (ḥijāb) . . . (33:53)**

The historical occasion for this revelation is clear. In Madinah, the need had arisen to protect the household of the Prophet, who had now become head of State, from easy informal access by each and everyone. This was done separating the official and the private quarters which has since become routine in official residence. This division was achieved with the aid of a screen (*ḥijāb*), introduced at the time.

It is tragic to see the use to which this verse has been put during the course of Islamic history, including the perversion of the harem in the

---

7. In 1989, three Muslim girls were prevented from entering the Gabriel-Havez College in Creil (Oise) in France at the beginning of the school year because of their headscarves. There followed a public dispute regarding the question of whether secularism demanded the toleration of headscarves or should ban them. After even the wife of the French State president, the Moroccan King, the President of the EC and the Cardinal of Paris had become involved, the French Education Minister finally allowed 'Ā'ishah, Faṭimah, and Samirah to wear a headscarf in the classroom, but not the gymnasium, a decision reversed since then.

palaces of the sultans. Still today, full veiling of women in Saudi Arabia is justified by it: women, that way, do not leave their screened-off private quarters even when walking in the street.[8]

In contrast, the other two Qur'anic verses mentioned establish a permanent dress code for woman per se.

> **O Prophet! Tell your wives and your daughters as well as all believing women that they should draw over themselves some of their outer garments (*min jalābibihinna*); this will help to assure that they will be recognized (as decent women) and not be annoyed. (33:59)**

It is significant that this regulation does not require that (i) the woman should first wear a certain article of clothing (e.g., a large headscarf) and (ii) then pull this down over her breast. The Qur'an assumes that women wear an article of clothing that allows the covering of their breasts, and that *this* is done.

In ancient times, this article of clothing would naturally have been worn over the head, at least in hot, windy, and dusty countries. However, a Qur'anic requirement for this cannot be derived from 33:59 with sufficient certainty.[9]

The last of these Qur'anic regulations discusses the protective purpose of the clothing regulations in more detail:

> **And tell the believing women to lower their gaze and guard their private parts and not to display their charms (*zīnatahunna*) beyond what may (decently) be apparent thereof (*illā mā ẓahara minhā*). So let them draw their head coverings (*khumūr*) over their bosoms. (24:31)**

The first two rules—that one should not eye the opposite sex in a provocative or suggestive manner and that one should hide one's *primary* sexual parts—are also imposed on men with the same wording (24:30).

---

8. The historic occasion for *āyat al hijāb* is well described in *Ṣaḥīḥ al Bukhārī*, hadith no. 6315. Seeking to emulate the Prophet is, of course, good practice. However, in my view, a regulation as described in 33:53, introducing a privilege in favor of the Prophet and a duty for his wives, Mothers of the Faithful (*Ummahāt al mu'minīn*), does not lend itself to emulation.

9. An interpretation to the other extreme is given in Saudi Arabia where 33:59 is read to require drawing the outer garment over the *entire person;* see "The Significance of Hijab," editorial in *The Islamic Future*, Riyadh, vol. XIII no. 69 (1997).

Close analysis shows that the third rule, i.e., that a woman should only show those parts of her physical 'charms' (her secondary sexual characteristics) which are normally visible anyway (*mā ẓahara minhā*), is a very sensible regulation: It takes into account that from period to period and from culture to culture there are great differences in the view of what, aside from her genitals and breasts, is erotic about a woman. This can be, but does not have to be, her feet, navel, voice, buttocks, or hair.

Therefore, with regard to the veiling of women, the Qur'an, within limits, makes allowance for cultural differences. The intentional ambiguity of the clause *illā mā ẓahara minhā* allows for adaptation to some aspects of the moral and social development of humanity.[10]

As rector of the Great Mosque in Paris, Sheikh Tedjini Haddam formulated the same view in an interview for Le Monde on 24. October 1989:

> Islam recommends that a woman be decently dressed, above all, that she cover that which *may* be her most attractive feature, her hair . . . Where this recommendation is to be applied depends on the social environment (translation and italics by the author).

Thus according to a minority of scholars the rationale of the clothing regulations of *Sūrat al Nūr* (24): 31, can be served without covering the hair when and where—as in northern Europe and North America—men are used to it and no longer particularly excited by its exposure. However, Islamic orthodoxy does not yet make allowances for different conditions that may exist within particular regions of the Islamic world. Majority view remains that a Muslim woman in public should be loosely covered—no 'tights'—and show of herself no more than her face, hands, and feet.[11]

In any case, wherever men still react to a display of women's hair, as a consequence of the uninterrupted practice of covering it, the covering of women's head hair obviously remains indispensable . This is the case in most regions of the Christian and Islamic mediterranean, where the covering of female hair has been traditional for centuries.

When two cultures clash over the matter of covering a woman's hair, the situation can become complicated as in the 'French hijab affair'.[12]

---

10. Muhamad Asad, *The Message of the Qur'an,* Gibraltar 1980, footnote 37 to 24:31; Prof. Rabah Stambouli, University of Algiers is of the same opinion, *HORIZONS,* Algiers 9/10/3. 1990, p. 5.

11. This is mainly based on a tradition related by 'Ā'isha, Abū Dawūd, hadith no. 4092.

12. See footnote 7.

'Ā'ishah, Fāṭimah, and Samīrah, who were asked by the French government to remove their scarves while they were at school, lived at home in an environment where a woman's hair is regarded as provocative; however, they participated outside the home in a culture that did not admit this to be so.

This is the doctrinal background for the phenomenon that some Muslim women show their hair and others don't.

Unfortunately, the headscarf dispute caused damage to Islam in the West because of the impression given that Islam is a rigid canonical religion geared towards, and politicizing, external matters, or that Muslims were confusing content and form, aim and method, spirituality and ritual.

It also caused damage within the Islamic community moving a secondary issue to center stage: People are now tempted to judge a *muslimah* merely on the basis of a headscarf, worn or not worn.

Therefore, it seems appropriate to end this chapter with a reminder: that veiling the face is not an Islamic invention, but rather one going back to the ancient Egyptian, Byzantine, and Iranian aristocracy, and that until recently even European women frequently wore a coquettish veil.[13] We should also remember that in the early nineteenth century, the Italian ballerina Marie Taglioni still caused a scandal when she dared to appear on the Paris opera stage with the hem of her long romantic skirt shortened by a few inches, showing a bit more than her anklets. . .

It is as important to allow European Muslim women, who have chosen the headscarf or the veil, to speak. These women unanimously point out that Western woman has become a sex object through a gradual process of undressing, and is under constant pressure to undress even more and to dress more provocatively.

The Western Muslim woman, who wears a headscarf or veil out of religious obedience, wants peace on the streets. She is trying to be pleasing in the sight of God; but she is also trying to escape the vicious circle I have described and to reestablish her dignity as a woman who as a wife reserves herself for her husband and does not want to appear as if she were still looking out for a husband. Muslim women with a headscarf are saying: Please, look at my face, not my legs!

---

13. See amongst others Noria Allami, *Voilées, dévoilées,* Paris 1989 for the opinion of an Algerian woman of the resistance generation.

Regarded in this way, wearing a veil is not a return to ancient Bedouin reflexes, to preserve the purity of the family tree, but a social protest against the degeneration of social life in contemporary Europe.

CRIMINAL LAW

OR

THE EXECUTION OF A PRINCESS

This book would not need a chapter on matters of criminal law if it were not for the fact that anti-Islamic forces enjoy serving up horror stories about Islam. They describe it as a religion in which hands are constantly being chopped off and women eagerly stoned.

Like any other State, Islamic States have always claimed the right to respond to acts that appear to deserve punishment by enacting legislation which complies with the Islamic point of view and that tradition into account, whether the crimes are against God, the community, or another person.

This man-made criminal law can be changed at any time, that is, it can move with the times, which is not quite the same as automatically adapting to the *zeitgeist.*[1]

However, the freedom to pass laws runs into limitations set by Qur'anic criminal laws because divine law takes precedence. A legal matter that is regulated by the Qur'an may not be regulated in any other way by legislation. Thus, a punishment foreseen by the Qur'an may not be increased, for this too would be human correction of God's command. And an immoral action for which the Qur'an—while dealing with it does not foresee punishment in this world, should not become an offense in any Islamic penal code. (Alas, as we shall see, both of this has actually happened.)

The Qur'an demands punishment for only six offenses, although it condemns many other types of misbehavior, from gambling to the consumption of pork, behavior which is threatened with consequences in the Afterlife. These six offenses are:

• Murder (*qatl*);[2]

---

1. On the subject of Islamic criminal law in general, see Konrad Dilger, "Das islamische Strafrecht in der modernen Welt," in *Weltmacht Islam,* Munich 1988; Joseph Schacht, *An Introduction to Islamic Law,* Oxford 1964; Abdur Rahman I. Doi, *Shari'ah: The Islamic Law,* London 1984; al Nawawi, *Minhāj al Tālibīn,* Lahore 1914.

2. 2:178; 4:92; 5:32,45; 6:151. On murder of a tyrant see Qur'an 42:39–41.

- Street robbery (*qat' al tarīq*);[3]
- High treason (*al hirābah*);[4]
- False accusation of adultery (*qadhf*);[5]
- Adultery between people of good reputation (*zinā*);[6]
- Theft of a guarded object of value (*sariqah*).[7]

The first three crimes are punishable by death. Traditional legal theory regarded the fifth crime (adultery) as justification for death (by stoning) under certain circumstances. Theft may be punishable by amputation, in the first instance, of the right hand.

So, in fact, the Qur'an contains very little material concerning penal law; regulations relating to criminal procedure are even more rare. This allows Islamic jurisprudence, which, in a humanitarian spirit, accepts certain dire realities of human life, the necessary freedom to soften the potential impact of Qur'anic criminal law through devising a very strict and highly demanding criminal procedure with very short periods of statutory limitation and narrow rules of evidence.

This is one more reason for the already stated divergence of theory and practice in Muslim legal life.

The Qur'anic code of criminal procedure is rudimentary, its only subject being the law of evidence (with its principle of requiring the evidence of at least two, and in the case of sexual offenses, four witnesses).

With regard to the punishment of adultery, the Qur'an itself demands something which is well-nigh impossible to fulfill—unless adultery is purposely committed in fullview. Proof of adultery can only be provided by four male *eye-witnesses* of good reputation, all of whom risk flogging should only one of their testimonies collapse.[8]

Clearly, requirements and risks of this kind mean that accusations of adultery are extremely rare. Added to this is the fact that even the adulterers' confessions are not sufficient in themselves; the judge must try to make them withdraw their confessions. So, before a princess can be executed for adultery—as occurred during the 1980s in Jeddah—a couple must have virtually provoked the condemnation through a wilful public

---

3. This is subsumed under Qur'an 5:33f.
4. 5:33; on the subject of apostasy alone, see the chapter "Tolerance or Violence?".
5. 4:15; 24:4.
6. 17:32; 4:15; 24:2.
7. 5:38; 2:188.
8. 24:4; 4:15; the occasion for this ruling was the accusation against 'Ā'ishah after the so-called 'necklace affair'.

attack on the fabric of the Islamic social order by frivolous, public sexual intercourse. To such behavior the Qur'an adds what amounts to a footnote:

Indeed, for those who love to see immoral conduct spread among the believers will be severe punishment in this world and in the hereafter. (24:19)

Thus, the stoning of adulterers is anything but a feature of the Islamic world, and this will also hold true of the future, if the following doctrinal analysis gains ground: Stoning adulterers was the punishment proscribed in the Bible.[9]

Given that Muslims honor previous revelations, this brutal practice would have become part of Islamic law had it not been abrogated by the Qur'an in *Sūrat al Nūr* (24):2, unconditionally replacing the stoning of adulterers with the flogging of one-hundred stripes.

Nevertheless, throughout Islamic history, though infrequently, married Muslim adulterers were stoned the Biblical way, and that supported by a very weak traditional foundation. Muhammad had, indeed, ordered the stoning of *Jewish* adulterers in Madinah, according to *their* law.[10] Only once, did he also tolerate the stoning of a Muslim adulterer,[11] however, his companions could not recall the essential fact, whether this happened before or after verse 24:2 was revealed.[12] Inspite of this, the Caliph 'Umar not only ordered the stoning of married Muslim adulterers when there was clear proof (pregnancy or confession),[13] he even claimed that there was a *ayat al rajam* (verse of stoning) in the Book of Allah.[14]

Even if the mentioned event in question had been tolerated by the Prophet *after* the revelation of verse 24:2, in line with many other contemporary observers[15] I would continue to deny the death penalty for adultery, and that on the basis of the fundamental principle that the Sunnah cannot abrogate the Qur'an. Where the Qur'an, settling details, has unmistakably spoken, the Sunnah must be silent.

---

9. Deuteronomy, the 5th Book of Moses, chapter 22:20–22.

10. Abu Dawud, hadith no. 4433 and 4435.

11. Abu Dawud, hadith no. 4405; also see *Ṣaḥīḥ al Bukhārī*, trans. by M. Khan, hadith nos. 8.805 and 8.810.

12. *Ṣaḥīḥ al Bukhārī*, hadith no. 8.817.

13. *Al Muwatta'*, 41.1.6 and 8.

14. *Ṣaḥīḥ al Bukhārī*, hadith no. 8.817.

15. These include Muhammad Asad, A. Yusuf Ali, Sheikh Si Boubakeur, and Professors Hamidullah and Rabah Stambouli.

On the subject of 'chopping off hands,' verse 38 of *Sūrat al Mā'idah* says:

> **And as for the man who steals and the woman who steals, cut off the hand of either of them as a punishment for what they have done (and) as a deterrent ordained by God . . .**

This seems to be so plain that travelers through the Arab world must be astonished when they fail to find a single sinner who has sacrificed his hand in this way despite the fact that thieves exist everywhere. But this is not surprising when we understand the Islamic interpretation of this criminal offense; for in this respect, too, the legal system and the reality of life diverge.

In the first instance, theft in the Qur'anic sense refers only to the stealing of a well-guarded object of more than petty value. If opportunity has made a thief of a man, he is not regarded a thief. Even the Caliph 'Umar—not known for leniency—dismissed any accusation of theft in times of privation and dire need. This led to the evolution of the now dominant theory, according to which theft is denied if one has reason to accuse the State of making inadequate provisions for its citizens by tolerating bad economic and social conditions. Muhammad Asad dedicates an entire page to this issue in his commentary to 5:38, ending with the categoric statement:

> (The punishment) is only applicable within the framework of a fully functioning social system and not under any other circumstances.[16]

In order to understand the Qur'anic threat of punishment for theft, it is important to understand that it complements Islamic family and inheritance law. According to this, Muslim women tended to keep their wealth, including their dowry gift, about their person in the form of precious jewelry, as a kind of old-age insurance; for in the case of divorce, men under Islamic law have no obligation to pay for maintenance. Under these circumstances, theft endangers the very system of old-age 'insurance' in a peasant and nomadic world.

Theft is also an attack on one of the most important pillars of the Islamic economic and social system—private property, which enjoys the protection of the Qur'an.

---

16. Muhammad Asad, *The Message of the Qur'an*, Gibraltar 1980, p. 149 f., note 48.

The actual deterrent effect of amputating a hand—to which 5:38 refers—is certainly colossal, as street security in Saudi Arabia, by day and night, shows. But the question of whether it is an inhuman punishment (because it maims the criminal) remains. From an Islamic point of view, prison sentences (a basis for which cannot be found in the Qur'an), particularly the life-long 'holing up' of a person and the banishment of prisoners from society and family, are inhuman as well. And what could be more maiming and inhuman than capital punishment—taking not a hand but life—which is practiced in countries that like to take the moral high ground vis-a-vis Islam? In the last resort, it must be understood that Muslims still assume that divine commandments, even if they transcend human comprehension, are commandments and not mere 'recommendations'.

'HOLY WAR'

I could complete a chapter with this title in a single sentence: the concept of 'holy war' (*sacrum bellum*), even the term, does not exist in Islam.

But I cannot make it so easy for myself; for the phenomenon that is falsely described as 'holy war' by Western Orientalists did once exist in the Muslim world: a religiously motivated war of aggression, as was customary at the time.

To the very grave associated charge that Islam showed a structural aggressiveness and readiness to do violence, I could seek an easy way out by placing the problem on the level of linguistics, namely by referring to the many layers of meaning in the Qur'an for the word *jihad* which basically denotes 'effort'.

But what would I achieve by proving that the formula of *jihād fi sabīl Allah* (striving on the path of God) can also be understood to mean (by the Sufis, for example) a striving to achieve moral purification; that today 'greater *jihad*' is taken to mean the battle against ones own moral weaknesses and not against heathens and other idolaters. For these truths do not negate the fact that during the course of Islamic history *jihad* has also, even primarily, been understood as armed struggle. And this, too, has its basis in the Qur'an. In medieval times many people even regarded *jihad,* defined as 'fighting,' as an additional sixth pillar of Islam after the five basic canonical duties.

Father Hans Vöcking has recently drawn merciless attention to this, trying to construct a Catch-22 dilemma for the Muslims: 'Those who interpret Jihad only in terms of defensive war or as personal moral striving, are denying the Qur'anic evidence as well as the history of orthodox Sunni doctrine.'[1]

In other words, if a contemporary Muslim speaks out against aggressive warfare aimed at spreading Islam, he may be a peace-lover, but he is no Muslim. On the other hand, if he is a Muslim, then he has to comply with the allegedly bellicose verses of the Qur'an,[2] on which Vöcking's statement rests.

---

1. Hans Vöcking, 'Dschihad', in: *CIBEDO,* Frankfurt 1991, no. 1, pp. 17 ff.

2. An analysis of the image of Islam in the textbooks used in German schools, carried out by the Islamic Scientific Academy in Cologne (now Hamburg), showed that systematically the false impression was given that the Qur'an was primarily a book of war. See

And when the sacred months are over, kill the disbelievers wherever you may meet them, and take them captive, and besiege them, and lie in wait for them in every suitable ambush. (9:5)

O Prophet! struggle hard with the disbelievers and the hypocrites and be firm against them! (9:73)

Now when you meet in battle those who disbelieve, strike their necks . . . (47:4)

This method of extracting individual verses of the Qur'an without regard for their context, the history of their revelation and their interpretation by Muslims, in order to prove an Islamic duty to wage aggressive war, is as if one were to interpret Jesus' words 'I came not to send peace but the sword' (Matt. 10, 34) as proof of Christian belligerence.[3] (This would be easier still if we were to use martial quotations from Martin Luther.)

So what is the real Qur'anic basis for a Muslim law of war?[4]

Verses can be found throughout the Qur'an reflecting a duty to uphold peace, permitting only wars of defense. The earliest of these revelations reads:

Permission (to fight) is given to those against whom war is waged, because they suffer wrong and most surely God has the power to assist them (22:39)

This was followed by the even more fundamental regulation in 2:190:

And fight in God's cause against those who fight against you, and do not commit aggression . . .

Vöcking, Zirker, Tworuschka, Falaturi, *Analyse der katholischen Religionsbücher zum Thema Islam*, Braunschweig 1988; see also Michael Klöcker, 'Der Islam im Spiegel katholisch geprägter Bildungsvermittlung', in: *Gottes ist der Orient—Gottes ist der Okzident, Festschrift für A. Falaturi*, Cologne 1991, p. 525.

3. Fuad Kandil, *Frankfurter Allgemeine Zeitung*, 10 October 1990, also in *CIBEDO* 1991, no. 1, pp. 24f.

4. In general see Isam Kamel Salem, *Islam und Völkerrecht*, Berlin 1984, pp. 103ff.; Hans Kruse, *Islamisches Völkerrecht*, 2nd edition Bochum, 1979, pp. 44ff.; Muhammad Sa'id R. al Būṭī, *Jihad in Islam*, Damascus 1995; Fathi Osman, *Jihad*, Los Angeles 1991; AbdulHamid A. AbuSulayman, *Towards an Islamic Theory of International Relations*, especially pp 19 ff. and 135.

It is only *after* this that the Qur'an continues:

> **And kill them wherever you may come upon them, and expel them from wherever they may have expelled you, for oppression is worse than killing ... (2:191)**

The prohibition of aggressive war is confirmed again and reinforced in a later revelation:

> **.. if God had willed to make them stronger than you, they would certainly have made war on you; thus, if they withdraw from you and do not fight you, and offer you peace, God does not allow you to harm them (4:90)**

And for good measure let us quote the 8th verse of *Sūrat al Mumtaḥinah* (60):

> **God does not forbid you to respect and be kind to those who do not make war against you on account of your religion, and do not evict you from your homes. . .**

Given this fundamental duty to keep the peace and this fundamental disapproval of wars of aggression, the verses selected by Father Vöcking are to be interpreted in a quite different way. They refer, as Muhammad Asad pointed out with conclusive logic as early as 1980, to a war which is already taking place, i.e., not to the right to start war (*ius ad bellum*) but to rules for conducting a war which has already broken out (*ius in bello*).[5]

It is absurd to imply that the Qur'an could give contradictory instructions on how to proceed on the issue of warfare!

It is also absurd to assume that the Qur'an—as interpreted by Vöcking—might encourage Muslims to sneak around in times of peace, a knife between their teeth, on a bloodthirsty headhunt for heathens!

And it is absurd as well to believe that the Qur'an would reject individual conversion by force (2:256) but encourage mass conversion to Islam by war.

---

5. See Muhammad Asad, *The Message of the Qur'an*, Gibraltar 1980, footnotes 167 and 168 to 2: 190, footnote 7 to 9:5, footnote 40 to 9: 29 and footnote 4 to 47: 4.

In view of such clear Qur'anic statements it is not necessary to tie one-self in knots because of what the Islamic jurisprudence during the Middle Ages had to say on the subject. It reflected the mores of its time and—once again—when the Qur'an has spoken so clearly there is no place for seemingly contrary arguments based on tradition. At any rate, war in the era of atomic, biological and chemical weapons and sophisticated, 'smart' weapons technology has assumed a character that allows us to consider all earlier theoretical discussions on the matter—whether by Catholic scholastics, like their theory of just war (*justum bellum*), or by Islamic scholars—as obsolete more likely than not.[6]

No one would deny that in Islamic and Occidental history, many bar-baric wars of aggression were fought on both sides in the desire of both worlds to conquer the world, although it is not true to say that the mas-sive initial success of the Islamic expansion is to be attributed to 'fire and the sword'. The Prophet of Islam, at any rate, derived justification for his campaigns or raids—even if some were offensive in the *tactical* sense—from a situation of *strategic defense,* in accordance with the Qur'an. There is no historical uncertainty about the fact that it was heathen Makkah that began and continued the aggression against him and the other early Muslims in Madinah.

The remaining elements of the Islamic military law may be summarized quickly as follows:

- a Muslim community has the duty to arm itself adequately in times of peace in order to deter attack (8:60);
- even if allied States enter a war, conflicting treaties must be hon-ored, even vis-a-vis non-Muslim States (8:72, 3:28); this was a rev-olutionary innovation of the Qur'an.
- male Muslims are subject to military service and have a duty to par-ticipate in war (2:190, 193, 216; 4:95f.; 22:39); there is no possibil-ity of 'conscientious objection'.
- war between Muslims is absolutely prohibited (4:92);
- only *amīr al mu'minīn* (commander of the faithful), i.e., the ruling caliph, may issue a call to a defensive war in the sense of *jihad;*
- in war, the means employed must not be disproportionate to their purpose (2:193f.; 22:60);

---

6. Murad Hofmann, "Der Islam und die Bombe," *Al Islam,* Munich 1984, no. 3, pp. 13 f.

- noncombatants are to be protected; destructive economic warfare (e.g., destruction of the enemy's economic basis by destroying palm groves etc.) is not allowed;
- besieged people should be given the opportunity to accept Islam or to surrender without a fight before any attack;
- if the opponent desires peace hostilities must cease (8:61);
- Paradise is promised to martyrs (4:73).

A brief look at this chapter should allow the reader to form his own judgement about the fact that the second Gulf War of 1990-91 had nothing to do with Islam—nor with *jihad*.

INTERNATIONAL LAW

Any discussion of this subject must take into account that Western international law which claims global validity is actually very young with its very conception of universal inter-State norms. The law of nations as we know it was only initiated by Hugo Grotius from Delft who laid its foundations with his *Mare liberum* (1609) and his *De jure belli ac pacis* (1625).

This hour of birth of international law in the modern Western sense had to await the 'birth hour of the sovereign State' (August Freiherr von der Heyde, 1952) amidst a revival of natural law theories.

Before this the 'ancient', that is to say, the Roman (and Islamic) legal conception had dominated, according to which there is (only) a so-called *jus gentium:* common customs and morals binding all communities internally and externally.[1]

In this sense the Qur'an provides a particularly good foundation for

• the international law of contracts and treaties;

• the status of minorities, including the law of asylum; and

• the international law of warfare (described in the chapter on 'Holy War').[2]

The Qur'an highlights the principle that treaties must be adhered to (*pacta sunt servanda*), even those with non-Muslims.[3] *Sūrat al Mā'idah* even begins with the sentence: '**O you who believe! fulfill the obligations (treaties)!**' This prepared the ground for the flourishing trade which was never interrupted even during the Crusades, the Turkish campaigns into Central Europe or the era during which Muslim corsairs operated against Spain from Salé and Algiers.

Since every Muslim belongs to the Islamic community, (the Ummah), Islamic law defines foreigners as Non-Muslims. Non-Muslims are protected by the community if they are given asylum (protection by a any

---

1. See Friedrich Berber, *Lehrbuch des Völkerrechts*, Munich 1960, vol. 1, pp. 1–16.

2. On the subject of Islamic international law in general, see Isam Kamel Salem, *Islam und Völkerrecht,* Berlin 1984; Hans Kruse, *Islamische Völkerrechtslehre,* 2nd edition, Bochum, 1979 Imran Ahsan Khan Nyazee, *Theories of Islamic Law,* Islamabad 1994.

3. 5:1; 8:72; 9:4.

individual is binding on the entire community!). Valid asylum can be based on such protection (*amān*) or on submission pledged to the entire Ummah. Those who must be protected within an Islamic State (*dhimmis*) form their own religious community, self-administered and with a right to representation. They are exempt from military service, but pay a special per capita tax. As Christians or Jews they enjoy the right to free practice of their religion or profession, including the consumption of wine and pork. Their property is guaranteed. But they have no assured access to the civil service or the army and—just like anyone else—may be subject to clothing regulations for the purposes of identification. No pressure may be put on them to convert to Islam.[4]

This Qur'anic minority statute shows extreme tolerance. Similar legislation and practice were not found anywhere else, either in the seventh century or a thousand years later—we need only consider the fate of the Huguenots, the Salzburg Protestants, the Russian Jews, the Andalusian Muslims, or the Bosnian Muslims these days. Nor was Islamic law in point 'too good to be true'. The efficacy of the Islamic protection of minorities was proved by the flourishing life of Jewish communities throughout the Islamic world—from the Maghrib to the Yemen and Istanbul—right up to the twentieth century. The Spanish Jews, for whom Muslims were no unknown quantity fled to those places and to Turkish Saloniki when they were exiled at the beginning of the sixteenth century.

In Moroccan 'Royal towns' such as Fes, one can still observe that the sultans of all dynasties liked to settle their Jewish minorities in direct vicinity of the palace. In this spirit, King Hasan II every year invites Moroccan Jews, emigrated to Israel, to return to their ancestral homes.

The new developments, outlined above in the Western view of international law, met with reservations in the Islamic world, and that for two conceptional reasons.

First, as is the case with every great religion or ideology (except Judaism), Islam is universalistic. Muslims dream of and strive for a Muslim world, despite the fact that neither the Qur'an nor the Sunnah promise that there will be only Muslims at the end of the world—quite the contrary.[5]

---

4. In fact, some early Muslim commanders refused to accept wholesale conversions as unserious.

5. According to one of the Prophet's famous statements, Islam came into the world as a stranger and will become a stranger in it once again: *Ṣaḥīḥ Muslim* , hadith nos. 270–272.

This universalistic approach led to the development in Islamic jurisprudence of a theory of the State, but not a theory of States in the plural.
Starting point for categorizing the plurality of the world remained that
only two forms of State were actually possible: the realm of the one and
only Ummah (the abode of Islam) and the other, in principle hostile, not
(yet) Islamic realm (the abode of war).[6]

Such an approach not only excludes the idea of several co-existing sovereign Islamic States—as we are constantly reminded of by the Libyan
head of State—but also excludes equal relations between the Ummah and
non-Muslim States, and thus international law in the modern sense.

The realities of international life—the normative power of the factual—
very soon necessitated a reconciliation of theory and practice by means of
new legal constructions.

Taking as model the famous armistice agreement which the Prophet had
concluded with the Makkans near *al Ḥudaybiyah* two years before his
definite re-entry into Makkah (628), Muslim scholars came to regard at
least short-term treaties with hostile forces as permissible, which led to
the acceptance of a third possible realm, *dar al ṣulḥ* or *dār al 'ahd* (the
abode of treaties/compromise). The constitution dictated by the Prophet
for the city State of Madinah founded on the coexistence of Muslim and
Jewish tribes[7] also pointed in this direction.

Despite this the Sultans of the Ottoman Empire, as caliphs of the
Islamic world of their time, did not agree to subject themselves to
Western international law until 1856. This finally occurred when Sultan
Abdulmajid signed the Paris Treaty in 1856, after the Crimean War;
Turkey thus entered the 'concert of (equal) powers' first devised by
Prince Metternich.

Of course, Muslims are not expected to adhere to treaties as an obligation derived from international common law or from 'natural law'. For
them also the sentence *pacta sunt servanda* rest on divine law.[8] But this
is of no consequence from a practical point of view. As far as results are
concerned it is irrelevant whether a partner adheres to a treaty because of
domestic law—the *shari'ah* in the case of Muslims—or because of the
legal fiction of inter-State law based on 'natural law'.

---

6. This division of the world into *dar al Islam* and *dar al ḥarb* or *dar al kufr* (the abode
of disbelief) has no direct basis in the Qur'an. Reflecting realities typical of the Middle
Ages, this terminology is obsolete today.

7. See M. Hamidullah, *The First Written Constitution in the World,* Lahore, 3rd edition,
1975.

8. Qur'an 5:1.

Here we have a purely theoretical dispute similar to the one about the real foundations of human rights (see the chapter "Human Rights").

Nevertheless, it remains questionable whether one can speak of a particular Islamic international law in the proper sense. Such regional international law, specific to Islam, could however develop in line with the socialist precedent—as a (perhaps only transitional) regulation of the very specific relations between Islamic States as they now exist. These particular rules would remain valid until the longed-for reorganization of the Ummah into a unified commonwealth succeeds. Merely a dream?

WHEN DENIGRATION
BECOMES TRADITION

On 31 May, 1962, Adolf Eichmann, a former high official of the infamous Nazi 'Storm Troupers' (SS), was executed in Ramla, kidnapped in 1960 by the Israeli secret service from his domicile in Argentina, he had been sentenced to death for his role in the Holocaust.

Eichmann had been engaged in organizing the transportation of Jewish people to Nazi extermination camps during World War II. As a defense he alleged that he had never personally laid hand on any Jew nor killed anybody himself. Nevertheless, he received capital punishment for having been what in German since then has been called a 'Schreibtischtater,' i.e., somebody who from behind his bureau desk and through his advise or instructions becomes guilty of what others do—as a remote but very real cause, as a 'white collar' criminal.

The most prominent victim of such 'Schreibtischtater' activities is the Prophet of Islam, and this is a historical curiosity. Michael Hart in his 1978 list, *The 100: A Ranking of the Most Influential Persons in History,*[1] placed Muhammad number one because he was "the only man in history who was supremely successful both on the religious and secular levels." And yet, as Montgomery Watt put in *Muhammad at Mecca,* "none of the great figures is so poorly appreciated in the West as Muhammad.[2] Indeed, from John of Damascus (d. before 754 near Jerusalem) via Dante Alighieri—who consigned Muhammad to indescribable torture in the 9th level of his inferno—to Voltaire[3] and Salman Rushdie's *Satanic Verses*[4] it became a tradition to denigrate Muhammad in a fashion which knew no limits. As analyzed by Annemarie Schimmel, "more than any other historical personality, Muhammad aroused fear, hatred, even disdain in the Christian world." According to her this was due to the Christian's incapability "to comprehend that there should have come another religion, after Christendom, so much more incomprehensible since this was a religion active in this world

---

1. Michael Hart, *The 100. A Ranking of the Most Influential Persons in History,* New York, NY 1978, p. 33.
2. Montgomery Watt, *Muhammad at Mecca,* Oxford 1953, p. 52.
3. See Voltaire's theatre play, *Mahomet le Prophète, ou le Fanatisme.*
4. Salman Rushdie, *The Satanic Verses,* New York, NY 1989.

and politically successful, occupying a large part of the formerly Christian dominated Mediterranean basin."[5]

We knew all along that Muhammad, almost from the beginning, had been libeled and slandered, reviled and defamed, smeared and detested as a fraud, a hypocrite, a power-greedy sex maniac, an epileptic, in short, a false prophet who created a heresy from hear-say, the very anti-Christ, deserving the name once again used by Rushdie, "*Mahound* (monster)." But as a result of recent research by non-Muslims like Norman Daniel[6] and Ekkehart Rotter[7] we now know that much of this perennial Christian propaganda was conceived and formulated against better knowledge. Documentation from the early 13th to the middle of the 14th century offer ample proof of this depressing, disgusting situation. In particular, Peter the Venerable, Benedictine Abbot of Cluny, had access to a translation of the Qur'an into Latin, the earliest one, produced under him in 1143 by Robertus Ketenensis and Hermannus Damata.[8] It is therefore unforgivable that even the most basic tenet of Islamic dogma—the unicity of Allah and the humanity of Muhammad—for propaganda purposes was turned upside down. In fact, the *shahadah - Ia ilāha illa Allah Muhammadan rasūl Allah* - was rendered *non est Deus nisi Machometus* (there is no God but Muhammad). Who then, has been fraudulent?

I do not want to imply that there has been no change for the better since those really dark middle-ages. Indeed, we have seen a more sympathetic attitude toward Islam in general, and more appreciation for the historical Muhammad in particular, as evidenced by poets like Johann Wolfgang von Goethe and Thomas Carlyle as well as by writers like Rudi Paret,[9] Karen Armstrong,[10] William E. Phipps, and Neal Robinson.[11]

On the whole, however, anti-Muslim feelings have become so deeply ingrained in the Western mentality, that even today Western reactions to political events in the Muslim world cannot be satisfactorily explained, or

---

5. Annemarie Schimmel, *Und Muhammad ist Sein Prophet*, 1981, p.7.

6. Norman Daniel, *Islam and the West: The Making of an Image* (1960), Edinburgh 1993.

7. Ekkehart Rotter, *Abendland und Sarazenen, Das okzidentale Araberbild und seine Entstehung im Frühmittelater*, Berlin/New York 1986.

8. For more details about that earliest Qur'an translation consult the *World Bibliography of Translations of the Meanings of the Qur'an—Printed Translations 1515–1980*, IRCICA, Istanbul 1986, p. 285.

9. Rudi Paret, *Mohammed und der Koran*, Stuttgart 1957.

10. Karen Armstrong, *Muhammad: A Western Attempt to Understand Islam*, London 1991.

11. William E. Phipps, *Muhammad and Jesus—A Comparison of the Prophets and Their Teachings*, London 1996; Neal Robinson, *Discovering the Qur'an*, London 1996.

predicted, without the factor of Islamophobia created centuries ago. In this sense, John of Damascus, Peter the Venerable, and Voltaire have all been 'Schreibtischtater'—people remote in time sharing responsibility for ugly events today.

A typical recent example is the fate of Bosnia-Hercegovina. My thesis is that the failure of the West in this tragic context was largely, if unconsciously, due to the described unfortunate heritage of Muslim denigration and misrepresentation.

A bit of factual history ought to substantiate this viewpoint. With the end of the Cold War around 1990, parts of the European world quite naturally moved from an ideological era into an era of chauvinistic nationalism. This was particularly true of the former Soviet camp. With the collapse of the post-Stalinist empire many peoples formerly held together ideologically (and by force) emancipated themselves on an ethnic, linguistic or 'national' platform. White Russia, the Ukraine, the three Baltic States, Moldavia, and the new, old States in the Caucasian region are good examples; so is former Yugoslavia. However, while all Western powers welcomed the disintegration of the former Czarist-Soviet colonial empire, most of them did not readily accede to the disintegration of Yugoslavia. At first sight a curious difference. After all, Tito's Yugoslavia, too, had only held together in the past by Communist ideology (and the fact that Tito while acting like a Serb was Croatian by descent) Also, it was clear that within Yugoslavia only Serbia and Montenegro remained Communist while the other federal republics—Slovenia, Croatia, Bosnia-Hercegovina and Macedonia—discarded Communism at the earliest opportunity. Finally, ever since 1986 it was clear to all who wanted to know that Serbia was out to establish the "national and cultural integrity of the Serbian people regardless of the republic or region in which Serbians live."[12]

Indeed, Slobodan Milosevic leader of the Serbian Communist Party (but of Montenegran origin), since that very year had already begun to persecute the Hungarian population of the Voyvodina and the Albanian population of Kosovo, virtually abolishing their autonomy already in 1989. As part of the same scheme, already in August 1990 the Serbian population in the Krajina region of Croatia declared their autonomy.

In response to these frightening developments, the populations of Slovenia, Croatia, Macedonia and Bosnia-Hercegovina decided to break away from Belgrade and to set up their own independent States. In Slovenia, on 23 December 1990, no less than 88% of the population voted for independence. On 19 May, 94% of the Croats followed suit.

---

12. *Memorandum of the Serbian Academy of Science,* September 1986.

Thereupon, Slovenia and Croatia declared themselves independent on 8 September 1991. Macedonia followed on 20 November.

Why then did powers like France and Great Britain continue to favor Yugoslav unity? Did the non-Serbian republics and regions not have every reason for breaking away and defending themselves against Serbian chauvinism? The answer is rather stark: The powers named, and others as well, were motivated by fear of each other and of a Muslim State in Europe, and by jealousy as well. In particular, they did not like the prospect that Germany—just reunited—would regain its former position of influence, and its market domination, in the area. The Allied suspicions regarding Germany seemed to come true when the Federal Republic—fully isolated—favored early official recognition of the breakaway republics. Bonn had not only understood that Yugoslavia could no longer be held together, the Germans believed that the ongoing Serbian aggression against Slovenia and Croatia (which had started immediately after their declaration of independence) could only be stopped effectively if it ceased to be treated as the 'internal affair' of defunct Yugoslavia. Germany, going alone, recognized Slovenia and Croatia, later than she had wanted—on 23 December 1991—but pointedly before the European Union (15 January 1992)—but too late for the Croatian martyr city of Vukovar which had already fallen to Serb soldateska.

The German position was logical but flawed in its execution because Germany herself was unwilling to support the new republics militarily, and her Allies were as unwilling. As a result, Milosevic was right in concluding that he had little to worry when continuing his drive to unite all Serbs in Croatia and Bosnia under his mythological Greater Serbian umbrella.

By that time, NATO, collectively, and its member nations, individually, had already missed the opportunity of terminating Balkan hostilities from the outset. Earlier, one single pin-point air attack on strategically important targets within Yugoslavia combined with a clear message and threat of further escalation would have done the trick. The Serbs would have understood immediately that the dire consequences of war would come home to them, and that they would be denied the luxury of fighting their war in other peoples territories. Needless to say, such incisive military action would have been covered by international law.

These opportunities having been missed, the chances of Bosnia-Hercegovina escaping Serbian aggression diminished drastically. On 29 February, 1992, 99% of the voters in Bosnia-Hercegovina voted for independence. The Serbian minority (31.3% at the time) had boycotted the referendum. When the European Union on 7 April officially recognized the

Republic of Bosnia-Hercegovina as an independent State, admitted by the United Nations only a few weeks later, the Serbian minority reacted by declaring their own independence. This is when Pale assumed the role of a 'capital' and Dr. Radovan Karadjic and General Mladic, later hunted as war criminals, emerged.

The terrible sequence is well known: Serbian rebel troops, reinforced by the official army of Serbia (JNA), occupied more than two-thirds of the country, massacring, torturing, raping, engaging in 'ethnic cleansing,' and destroying every mosque and Roman Catholic church in sight.[13] No similar crimes had been committed on European soil since Stalin and Hitler. 'Ethnic cleansing' on religious grounds had last been practiced on Muslims by the Most Catholic King and Queen of Spain in the early 16th century.

And yet, the 'civilized world' did not intervene militarily. Instead, it engaged in humanitarian aid, making sure that the Muslims, while being tortured, at least would not be hungry. Instead of forcing their way into Sarajevo, besieged and bombarded for three years, NATO planes established an air bridge, interrupted whenever the Serbs pleased to do so. UN 'peace keeping forces' were dispatched into a country where there was no peace to be kept. Their mandate allowed them to be shot at but hardly ever to retaliate. In 1995, it became horribly clear that the U.N. were not even resolved to defend their 'security zones' in Srebrenica and Zepa. Worse, by maintaining an arms embargo not only against the aggressor but against his victim as well—from July 1992 to the end of 1995—the 'Family of Nations' deprived one of them of its right to self-defense. During most of this time, UN and European mediators like Cyrus Vance, Lord Owen, Stoltenberg and Bildt tried to achieve peace by honoring most of the war gains the Serbians had made, all the while claiming that "only a political solution" was possible. In fact, they and the so-called Bosnia Contact Group pressured the Bosnians and Croatians into accepting an unfair splitting of the country, giving 51% of the territory to 61% of the population (Muslims and Croatians) and 49% to the Serbs (31%).

The Bosnian Serbs, however, against the advise of Milosevic, the strategist, wanted even more, in particular Sarajevo itself. (Before the war, it had been a city with very few Serbs.) This was a mistake. The exasperated world now accepted that Croatia retook its Krajina region by force. And televised horror images from Sarajevo finally moved the United States

---

13. In Amir Pasic, "Islamic Architecture in Bosnia and Hercegovina," *IRCICA*, Istanbul 1994, out of 591 noteworthy examples of Islamic architecture there, 349 have been severely damaged or totally destroyed deliberately either by Serbian or Croatian forces.

into action. From 30 August to 14 September 1995, NATO fighter planes at last did what they could have, and should have, done all along: Bombard Serbian military targets, at least within Bosnia. Even the Muslims were now able to regain some ground, particularly around Bihac.

Decisive military action, and nothing else, moved Serbia and even the Bosnian Serbs finally into accepting a peace arrangement *in their favor,* negotiated in Dayton (Ohio) from 1 to 21 November and signed in Paris on 14 December, 1995. Its execution will virtually split Bosnia into two. It is only a question of time when the "Bosnian-Serbian Republic" within the new State will quit it in order to join Serbia proper, as envisaged all along. The remaining 'Bosnian-Croatian Federation,' however, will no longer have a chance to establish an Islamic Republic, as envisaged by Alia Ali Izetbegovic. This 'Islamic threat' has been effectively prevented from realization at Dayton.

So much for the pathetic facts, and now some analysis.

By the time the peace treaty was signed in Paris, 200,000 people had been killed, three million driven from their homes, tens of thousands of women had been raped, and a hundred thousand buildings destroyed, right in the center of Europe and under the noses of major 'civilized' powers.

Their incredible inactivity demands a rational explanation because States normally do not act irrationally. The first question to be raised in this context relates to major misjudgments of which Western governments were guilty right from the outset: about the chances of keeping Yugoslavia together, and about the nature of the war.

Anybody studying sentiments at Belgrade when Tito was still alive and active would have had a foretaste of what would happen once Yugoslavia's common denominators—Tito and Communism—frittered away. Even then, the near fanatic dislike of each other—Croats and Serbs—was as clear as daylight: It is an enmity not based on (nonexistent) differences of ethnicity or language but on different cultural identities. The Croats are Roman Catholic, thus oriented toward Rome and using Latin script; in the past, they were allied with Austria-Hungary against the Ottoman Empire. The Serbs, however, are Greek-Orthodox, thus oriented originally towards Constantinople, later toward Kiev and Moscow, and using Cyrillic script; they had been subdued by the Turks for some 450 years, ever since the legendary battle on Kosovo Palje in 1389—an event whose memory Serbian folklore has deeply anchored in the Serbian psyche as a tragic disaster demanding revenge.

Slobodan Milosevic raised Serbian chauvinism to a pitch in an anniversary speech at Kosovo Polje on 21 June, 1989, 600 years after the event, starting to destroy the delicate balances both within Serbia and within Yugoslavia. Slobodan in clear daylight was engaged in destroying Yugoslavia. Why would well-informed Western governments not see this? The only plausible answer is that they could not see what they did not want to see, being victims of wishful thinking. They badly wanted things to be all quiet on the southeastern front.

They also misjudged the very character of the war, treating it as a tribal conflict typical of the Balkans where—don't we all know?—everybody usually fights everybody, where all are unreasonable, and where guilt is always equally spread among all parties. A thoroughly contemptuous view indeed

In reality, it had been clear ever since the anti-Turkish (i.e., anti-Muslim) pitch of Milosevic's anniversary speech that the Serbs were about to launch a new crusade. Serbian officials, media, Serb-Orthodox clergy as well as Greek media were astonishingly outspoken about the purpose of the 1992-1995 Balkan war. For them it was all about "eliminating the last Muslim pocket in Europe," no more and no less. In other words, what we witnessed in Bosnia at the end of the 20th century, seen through Serbian and Greek eyes was nothing other than a religious war, thus bound to be particularly savage.

Why did Western governments fail to grasp that point? To that question, there is more than one plausible explanation. Certain Western actors refused to believe that religious wars still were possible. Many of them, being themselves utterly irreligious, could not even imagine that religion still can be a potent political agent. But more often their perception was disturbed by preset ideological ideas about inevitable human progress which simply did not admit the notion of religious warfare in our time. No, according to them, the Middle Ages simply had to be behind us.

At the outset, and up to 1991, these were perhaps understandable mis-calculations. But why did the West not interfere decisively when, as of 1992, it had become glaringly obvious that the Serbs were slaughtering Muslims in a new holocaust?

It can be automatically excluded that Western governments are inept at crisis management. In particular, NATO countries have highly developed procedures and doctrines for crisis control. Annual NATO-wide staff maneuvers like HILEX[14] and WINTEX[15] have helped to refine the lessons previously learned. Thus NATO governments know, for instance, that conflict termination through controlled escalation and de-escalation is an art

14. HILEX stands for High Level Exercise.
15. WINTEX stands for Winter Exercise.

where all depends on clear statements of intent well communicated to the adversary. In this context, it is known to be of the essence that military threats must be seen both as sincere and limited, giving the adversary no more reaction time than absolutely needed for reflection and execution.

Alas, during the Bosnian war Western actors violated each and every rule they had learned and rehearsed during their exercises. Unclear threats were made. Worse, such threats were linked to time limits so extended that the Serbs could decipher them as not serious or take the necessary countermeasures.

The mistakes made in the cases of Srebrenica and Zepa were revolting. First, against clear evidence, it was questioned whether Serbian forces were moving forward. Then, when they had sufficiently moved forward, possible air intervention was rightly considered too late. U.N. forces even allowed the Serbs to take back military hardware, which earlier they had delivered in accordance with UN resolutions. The result of all these tactical mistakes was that the United Nations and the Western Alliance lost much credibility. And without credibility crisis management is virtually impossible.

Western actors being neither stupid nor inept: Why did they act as if they were inept?

There is a benign and a less benign explanation. The simplest (and benign) explanation is that the West acted egotistically, just as can be expected from thoroughly materialistic societies unwilling to sacrifice, especially for those "barbaric tribes far away in the dark Balkans". True, intellectually, many realized that action was necessary. But they found themselves emotionally unable to act: A symptom typical of decadence.

Indeed, this Western attitude recalls similar Occidental inaction in the face of the Ottoman siege of Constantinople in 1453. The Byzantine emperor, like Izetbegovic, strongly appealed for help to the Western powers, who at that time were the Pope, Venice, the German emperor, and the kings of France and England. As in the Bosnian case (1992–1995), the medieval Western powers replied that a political solution should be sought with Sultan Mehmet II. They also argued that East Rome was far away, thus intervention would be very costly and anyway probably too late. When the Pope finally decided to rent a few frigates from Venice for the defense of Byzantium, the Venetians coolly reminded him that he had not yet paid the last rental contract.[16]

---

16. Steven Runciman, *The Fall of Constantinople,* 1453, London 1964.

Curiously enough, Western populations can be mobilized for faraway 'good causes,' be it a jailed Chinese dissident, the nonsinking of a Shell oil platform, or the prevention of nuclear tests in the South Pacific—provided that the media popularize such issues dear to Green Peace or Amnesty International. Of course, it is disputable whether or not the French tests in the Pacific will cause damage to the environment; but it is indisputable that 200,000 people were actually—not potentially—killed in Bosnia and Croatia NOW.

Why would Green Peace and A.I. not act decisively against Serbia? Was it the Bosnian Muslims fault that they have no oil? That they are human-beings instead of whales, deserving preservation? Or that they are Muslims? In spite of what has been advanced above, Western governmental inaction does remain puzzling because Western media, particularly in Germany and France, did not fail to bring the cruelties and absurdities of the war situation into the living rooms at home.

This prompts me to submit the lesser benign interpretation of Western tactics:

Deeply rooted anti-Islamic feelings. To understand this, let us go back again to the siege of Constantinople in 1453. At that time, too, Western disinterest in Byzantium was principally rooted in religious prejudice: the East Romans, the Greek-Orthodox, refusing to unite with Rome, were considered in the West as damned heretics who basically deserved to be conquered and punished by Fatih Sultan!

I am fully convinced that the Western failure to act in favor of the integrity of Bosnia has been similarly motivated, and here is the acid test: Suppose the Serbs were Muslims and the Bosnians were Catholics. Now suppose that these Muslim Serbs had acted exactly as the actual Serbs have done during the last five years. In this situation, can anyone imagine the West not coming down on the Serbs, from the very outset, like a ton of bricks? NATO countries would indeed have considered it their Christian-Humanitarian duty to rescue the Bosnian Christians from such barbaric Muslim aggression and persecution. Can anyone imagine that the West, in such a case, would have punished the Christian Bosnians with an arms embargo, abandoning them to the massacre of 'fanatic' Muslims? In fact, the answer in each case is no.

Deep down—as a relic from centuries of Christian anti-Muslim propaganda, denigration of Muhammad, and Muslim-Christian warfare—the average Western actor has no sympathy whatsoever for the prospect of an Islamic State in Central Europe. On the contrary, he is afraid of it.

The belated bombing of the Serbian position by NATO forces in fall of 1995 is no evidence to the contrary. This action was not taken in favor of the Muslims but out of frustration with the Bosnian Serbs. They were bombed into accepting a peace treaty *in their own favor* (and to the detriment of the Muslim side).

Of course, the Muslim world—O.I.C. and Arab League—could have been more energetic in their efforts to help Bosnia. It must, however, be seen that much more help was indeed given than is known because the arms embargo did not allow official military aid. For a time, Turkish as well as Saudi newspapers carried frequent death notices of Muslim legionaires killed in action in Bosnia. Nevertheless, one cannot help feeling that the Bosnians at the beginning were not fully accepted as 'real Muslims' by all concerned, if only because they did not say frequently enough *in shā'a Allah, mā shā'a Allah,* and *al ḥamdu li-lLah.* But who was to judge except Allah *ta'ala*? And who had read Alia Ali lzetbegovic's publications—his *Islamic Manifesto* and *Islam between East and West,* proving him to be one of the most original (*Salafi*) thinkers of Islam, and a man of profound spirituality and education?[17] At any rate, many a Bosnian today is more conscious and "practicing" a Muslim than he had been under Communist rule.

As long as the Western mentality suffers under its historical prejudices against Islam, Bosnia will not be the last "Bosnia". Indeed, even before the 1995 armistice in Bosnia-Hercegovina another Muslim people were massacred, this time in Chechnya. Its people had fought for the preservation of their Islam under Imam Mansur in the 18th century and Imam Shamyl in the 19th century. Today they fight again, with incredible sacrifices and with incredible determination. And again, as during the by-gone centuries, the Chechnians are victims of their faith, and entirely on their own. Only today, their oil and gas riches work even more against their aspirations. The West—alas, the Muslim world as well—stands by, allegedly for reasons of State (territorial integrity; public order). But deep down, I bet, one finds, there as well, a historically nourished fear of a development that might lead to a Caucasian *Islamic* Federation (between Chechnya, Dagestan, Abhaziya, Circassia, lnguchiya, and Ossetiya).[18]

These and other atrocities may happen again anytime, anywhere, wherever denigration of Islam has become tradition.

---

17. Alia Ali Izetbegovic, *Islam Between East and West,* American Trust Publications, Indianapolis, 2nd ed. 1989.

18. Muhammad Iqbal Khan, *The Muslims of Chechnya,* The Islamic Foundation, Markfield, Leiceistershire 1995.

GLOSSARY*

Ash'arīyah
Ninth century school of philosophy famous for its rigid epistemology, founded by Abu al Hasan al Ash'arī (874–935) in opposition to that of the Mu'tazilah school (see below); philosophical basis of orthodox Sunni Islam.

Bid'ah
Prohibited innovation in the theological and legal domain.

Caliph
(Arabic *khalīfah*, pl. *khulafā'*) Representative of the Prophet (not of God) after his death, but without a prophetic mission. The spiritual and secular head of the Ummah.

Dhikr
(Arabic lit. 'remembrance') Prayer technique of constant repetition, often used in Islamic mysticism.

Dhimmī
Member of a protected minority in an Islamic State.

Fiqh
Islamic jurisprudence.

Ḥadith
A tradition of the Prophet.

Ḥajj
The fifth pillar of Islam, consisting of acts performed by pilgrims in and around Makkah on the ninth and tenth days of Dhu al Ḥijjah, the last month of the Islamic lunar year.

Ijtihad
Effort to solve legal issues, based on the legal sources of Islam.

---

* For more detailed definitions consult Ruqaiyyah Waris Maqsood, *Islam—A Dictionary*, Cheltenham, U.K. 1996; Ahmad von Denffer, *Kleines Wörterbuch des Islam*, Lützelback 1986; Gibb/Kramers, *Shorter Encyclopaedia of Islam*, Leiden 1974; Muhammad Ahmad Rassoul, *Der deutsche Mufti*, Cologne 1997; Thomas P. Hughes, *Dictionary of Islam* (1886), Chicago 1994.

Integrism
Opposition to secularism within the Islamic world.

Islamism
(Arabic *Islāmīyah*) Term for Islamic reform movements of the twentieth century which emphasize political aspects of Islam.

Jāhilīyah
Pre-Islamic period of ignorance in Arabia, to which Islam brought
about an absolute caesura.

Jihad
Self-exertion in the cause of Allah. Falsely translated in the West as
'holy war'.

Kharijites (*Khawārij*)
The oldest religious sect in Islam. A puritan, democratic sect that arose
in the seventh century through a secession (Arabic root *kharaja*) from
both Sunni and Shi'i Islam.

Laylat al Qadr
'Night of Power,' at the end of the month of Ramaḍān, probably in the
year 610, in which the Prophet Muhammad received his first revelation,
verses 1–5 of *Sūrat al 'Alaq* (96).

Mu'tazilah
Speculative rationalist Islamic school of philosophy of the ninth century which emphasized man's freedom of will.

Qur'an
Holy Book arranged in 114 *sūrahs* (chapters) containing the revelations
of Islam that the Prophet Muhammad received from God Almighty over
the course of 22 years.

Salah
Ritual prayer. The supreme act of worship in Islam, held daily at five
times.

Shari'ah
Collective name for all the laws of Islam, including Islam's whole religious, liturgical, ethical, and jurisprudential systems.

Shi'ah
Supporters of the Party of 'Ali; today found especially in Iran, Iraq, the
Lebanon, Azerbaijan, and the Gulf.

Shūrā
Political decision making procedure, required by the Qur'an, through common or representative consultation.

Sīrah
Life of the Prophet Muhammad, also biography of the Prophet.

Sufism
Islamic mysticism.

Sunnah (of the Prophet)
The Prophet Muhammad's exemplary way of life as documented in the canonical collections of reports (ḥadith, pl. *aḥādith*) on what he said, did and allowed.

Sunni
Majority Islam (c. 90 percent); distinguished from Shiʻah.

Taqlīd
In a figurative sense: blind imitation of recognized authorities in the legal and theological domain; opposite *ijtihad*.

Tawḥīd
Central Islamic doctrine of the Oneness of God; rejection of the Christian theories of the Trinity and Incarnation.

'Umrah
Lesser Ḥajj; short pilgrimage that can be performed throughout the year.

Ummah
Community of all Muslims that transcends State borders, nationalities, races and linguistic barriers.

Zakah (Zakat)
Wealth tax at the yearly rate of 2.5 percent, paid for the well-being of the poor, the needy, prisoners, charity, defense, administration, and the community.

INDEX